Dedicated to my parents:
Constant Georges MERITZA
(1929-2011)
Josiane MERITZA
(1936-)
and to the one who shares my life
my friend Sophie

Special thanks :

Yoann MERITZA

THE MIND
ABOVE
THE LINE

FSC
www.fsc.org
MIXTE
Papier issu
de sources
responsables
Paper from
responsible sources
FSC® C105338

Editor:

BoD-Books on Demand,

12/14 rond point des Champs Élysées

75008 Paris, France

Print: BoD-Books on Demand,

Norderstedt, Allemagne

legal deposit June 2018

ISBN : 9782322082308

cover picture :

license : cco 1.0 universal / (cco 1.0)

graphic design : Yoann MERITZA

The mind above the line

"I feel that my whole life depends on that moment. If I miss it ...

- I think the opposite. If we miss this moment, we try the next one, and if we fail we start again the next moment. We have all our life to succeed
(Boris Vian - "The foam of days")

"Courage is to act and to give oneself to great causes without knowing what reward reserves the deep universe for our effort, or whether it reserves a reward for it. "
(Jean Jaurès)

A FEW WORDS ABOUT THE AUTHOR

Yoann MERITZA is an essayist writer specializing in personal development, including NLP (Neuro Linguistic Programming), EFT (Emotional Freedom Therapy), and Behavioral and Cognitive Therapy. He has made himself known in over twenty countries thanks to his proven method, and brings together many followers of his philosophy of surpassing oneself. He is the author of "Guaranteed Success" and "How to reprogram his subconscious mind ?".

He was born March 28, 1978 in Bonneville in Haute-Savoie and grew up in Cluses in this same department. He studied accounting and a training of SME-SMI collaborator where he learned NLP (Neurolinguistic Programming). He has participated in many internships and seminars on communication and is passionate in the field of personal development. Self-taught in the soul, he continues to perfect himself in the communication and study of human nature following the footsteps of many authors of the same theme such as Napoleon Hill, Norman Vincent Peal, Florence Scovel Shinn or Dr. Joseph Murphy.

He creates his own method by synthesizing his many readings on the subject and brings readers to a broad understanding of the field of personal growth through a simplified approach for assimilation at all levels, his concern always being the accuracy of the theme chosen and to provide novice readers with clear and affordable answers at all cultural levels.

His father, Constant Georges, died on July 5, 2011 at the age of 81, was a model for him. He was a veteran of Indochina, and a former member of the TOE-GCI, road in the civil, was diagnosed with cancer of the throat in 1981, he always fought and had cultivated an enthusiasm despite his disability, because he understood how precious life was and how to live it intensely. He was a veteran both during the Indochina War, and fought for the rest of his life. He has always helped Yoann to stand up and overcome the trials of life.

Yoann bathed in this environment where he had to fight every day, he always tried to go ahead whatever happened and tried new experiences.

He attended normal schooling until 1993 before returning to apprenticeship school in Saint Jeoire where he discovered the trades of electrician, carpenter, bar turner and welder, which made him a "touch-to-do all ".

In September 1995, new turning point in his life, he followed a path in the tertiary accounting at Private Professional High School "the cordeliers" in Cluses, where he discovered the office and administrative, he also learned computer management that he still serves today in his private life. But missed his BEP by a few points.

Under the guidance of his former accounting professor, he retried his BEP in 1998, which he obtained.

From February 1999 to December of that year, he did his national service at Auxonne in Burgundy at 511th Train Regiment, then at 27th BCA at Cran-Gevrier in Haute-Savoie.

After leaving the army, he decided to try his BA in accounting as an independent candidate, he Bucha for months on all subjects, became his "own teacher," even today, autodidact at heart, he knew "self coach", he graduated, but decided not to stop, feeling grow wings, he worked in the industry to finance his studies by correspondence, which was for him "a big piece Every night to attend classes, but the results were slim for him.

He undertook to resume his studies in recurrent session in 2001, inquired at training centers and at the "Information and Orientation Center" (CIO) where he was followed by a counselor who helped him fill out the forms. necessary for his reintegration into the professional cycle.

In September 2001, he returned to the Lycée Guillaume Fichet, he was then 23, four years separated from other students, a slight generational shock that he was able to compensate, he adapted very well to this environment, and in June 2003 he obtained his professional bachelor's degree in accounting.

He tried all means to pass his BTS, because at 25, he was now too old for employers, as a professional immersion in two years. He suffered defeats, but did not admit defeat. He attended some seminars for major car brands, including Valence in the Drôme.

In 2004, he seized a golden opportunity by following a training of SME / SMI collaborator at the Chamber of Commerce and Industries of Scionzier in Haute-Savoie, he discovered the NLP (Neurolinguistic Programming) where he learned the tools to shape the subconscious, and manage human nature.

From 2007 to now, he has been interested in the topics of personal development, control of the subconscious and has read many books on the topics of psychology and behavior, he has also attended coaching seminars. He still follows, and quite regularly coaches in personal development.

He is also a member of the National Union of Combatants (UNC-Alps), and the friendly 27th BCA.

INTRODUCTION

Hello to you readers friends,

First of all, for those who do not know me yet, let me introduce myself.

I am, I was, and I will be, at the same time, an author, an actor, and a spectator like everyone else, and I will explain to you later why I say this.

I am Yoann MERITZA, author specialized in personal development, in particular in NLP (Neuro Linguistic Programming), EFT (Emotional Freedom Therapy), and in Behavioral and Cognitive Therapy. Human nature has become for me a source of inspiration and behavioral study fascinates me, because there is always matter to learn, because as a quote would say:

"The more we know, the less we know! "

I have already made my mark in social networks and I make myself known in more than twenty countries, especially in France, in Spain, and the United Kingdom, but this was a long way that was not often paved with gold.

As everyone started out in the field of personal growth and the study of human nature, and who became famous over the years, there was a starting point, these people were like you, they were like me, being part of the popular mass, but they have been able to stand out by winning and believing in their dreams, everyone has the right to succeed and deserve a better life. And as an author in personal development, I respect this concept enough because I know where I come from.

Authors like Max Piccinini, Franck Nicolas, Slavica Bobdanov, Jack Canfield, Bob Proctor and many others are people I respect a lot because they come from a so-called "popular" milieu, where you are right now, but look where they are now, they have succeeded brilliantly, and take pleasure in sharing, like me, their knowledge. Why would not it be the same for you? It also means that you doubt your ability, but you will learn that for those who really believe in it, anything is possible!

I hope that you, yourself, will break the barriers of your life, find your place in society, just as so many others have done, that is the purpose of this book, and I will give you all the tools you need to get there, but you have to work together, what you're going to discover is a very powerful way to get everything you want in life, but it's not a magic book, it calls for common sense and rules that govern the universe.

You hold in your hands the book of your life and believe it or not, something has led you to these lines.

How could I define this one? It's a collection of all the tools that can lead you to success on all levels, and be the person you've always wanted to be, and go beyond your wildest dreams, he holds the keys of a power, that of attraction.

If you do not believe for a moment, nothing prevents you from going further upstream of this reading, but it would be a shame to miss the opportunity to change all your destiny, to be "above of the line ".

Well used, this book has immense power, allowing you to cross barriers that seemed impossible to reach.

You still do not believe it? Let me prove you the opposite over the pages, I'll take you on a wonderful journey inside yourself, something will happen, "It will materialize as you progress through your reading! But I do not tell you what it is for now.

There is no magic in there, everything you want is happening, at any time, I will explain how.

This book will tell you everything you need to know about the law of attraction, it has been designed so that you understand in essence the essential rules of life to respect to make good use of it. Everything that you will discover there will exceed all your expectations by bringing clear answers on the subject, such is my objective by writing it.

It is the fruit of long hours of research work on the subject, I could say that it is a pure concentrate of knowledge, such was my will in writing it, it is to make it effective and it is, that said, do not expect that everything happens alone, it will be necessary to put of your, I give the bases of the foundation, with you to build what you want on it.

However, I want to warn you that if you apply everything you find there, it can affect your mind and your body, which will result in nausea, migraines, mood swings or vertigo, because it puts in opposition two types of thoughts and behaviors, yours in its current form, and those that you desire. It may shake you up.

It's a book that will take you where you want to go, provided you do not force the events, everything that's going to happen will have a direct impact on your day-to-day, so read it quietly. It gathers valuable information, resulting from many researches in the field, anecdotes and excerpts of articles, it is quite complete, at least for the author, you will make your own opinion.

Also understand the complexity of making such a book, many hours of writing, reformulations, liters of coffee, a few dozen used pens to get a pure concentrate (just two pens, I inflate a little thing !)

Important point: at the beginning of the transformation process, keep this for yourself, do not mention this book in any case, especially in your current environment, you are still novices for most and some people around you will not understand, very little in phase with this type of theories, but when the first changes are going to happen, that you will be convinced yourself that everything that is said in this book works, you can share it en masse.

You will improve beliefs about yourself, you will feel able to go beyond your dreams. Be patient, read this book quietly and great truths will be revealed to you, but all you need to know, if you follow all that you will see to the letter, you will evolve to a level, go a step above, a line separating your reality from that coveted. It is one of the most powerful forces of nature.

I do not let the suspense linger any longer, and I wish you good reading.

Sincerely

Yoann MERITZA
Specialized author

PART I:
LAW OF ATTRACTION

CHAPTER 1 :
WELL PREPARE HIS SPIRIT FOR THE LAW OF ATTRACTION

"To reach the end goal, I focus first on prepa-ration. "
(David Douillet)

The law of attraction is one of the most power-ful forces in the universe, but very few know how to use it. All that is noted in this chapter is above all common sense.

Like a magnet, it attracts to you everything you want in your life, but there are conditions for this law to be used optimally.

On New Year's Day 2017, I remember receiv-ing some notes from someone I did not know on a piece of paper, but I admit to being tempt-ed by what was noted above, that is, a few in-structions, and the woman I met that day told me that I would learn to use them the best way they are.

One question remained in me: "Why me? What more did I have that could differentiate me from others?

Later, I realized that I had nothing more than I already possessed, that is, "everything," as curious as it could be said.

In fact, we all have this power in us. Everything that happens in our lives comes from one place: ourselves!

The external conditions are a reflection of our inner world, and in reflecting, making a video recording of myself, I made a discovery.

By conditioning oneself to take a step back on one's own image, as if we see a person outside of our circle, we have what is called the "outside eye".

As amazing as it may seem, all the flaws I saw in others, I found them on this recording, I started to do my self-criticism. It opened my eyes to the person I was: "So this is how I am perceived? "

I invite you to experience it! Even if you do not recognize it right now, you have a lot of flaws, in fact, everyone has it, but also, everyone likes to lie to each other.

Bob Proctor, another self-developmental author, speaks of "attitude," but this is to understand in a broad sense, it is the attitude towards ourselves and others. The world around us is the strict reflection of who we are, the people we meet, the work we do, our housing and our way of life, everything is the same, and as the saying goes "that is alike s' together "!

It may not be the conditions that you want, but indirectly, you provoke them, I know very well that this is unenthusiastic, but it is the sad reality. I will detail a little further!

But it's a difficult concept to assimilate as long as we have blinders, prisoners of our beliefs.

Where do these beliefs come from? Directly from our childhood, and it is a set of neuro-associations that we made between an external element (words, colors, people ...), and our inner world. We are formatted from birth to have certain beliefs, by what is called the "paradigm". I will devote a whole chapter on this last point!

As I want everything that will be mentioned in this book to really work, and to show that the law of attraction is not a fantasy (you will discover it for yourself), let me give you some details for use it well.

Many have read a lot of books on the subject, without really knowing how to put the principles exposed in it, and yet, these books written by excellent authors, I can recommend some of them, Mickael Losier, Max Piccinini, Franck Nicolas, Napoleon Hill, Bob Proctor, Slavica Bogdanov and many others, have a very good approach to the subject. They are very competent in this area, and I invite you to read many of their books on the subject, you will discover points of similarities, and the advantage of knowing different visions of the law of attraction will allow you to understand explanations that are best suited for you.

That said, I want to give you some details about what you will discover over the pages, and use a great deal with you.

For my part, I have never hidden that it requires a constant investment on your part, we do not write books of magic (all authors combined), there is only one that is already in you. Power comes from within and not from outside, and what we do, we help you find that power, understand where it is in your mind, we open the path, you follow it.

To get everything you want in life, you need to fully invest!
What am I telling you? I'm just saying that everything that will be presented here in this book is largely a matter of common sense, I do not sell dreams, and I'm not a magician, and in these pages you will not find a way to do to appear a rabbit of a magic hat, it is not either an esoteric collection, you must first put feet on the ground. If these are the types of books you

were looking for, they are located in the "fantasy" department of your city library.

What is presented in this book is something a little more serious, it's about personal development, and it's used in communication expert firms to train salespeople for example, it brings a better vision on its own person and human nature in general.

Everyone has their own training technique, and for my part, I am an essayist author, that is to say that I bring a vision, not to say opposite, but the finality remains the same by having a subject approach quite different from what you know.

And as, as author, I really want to bring you the best and give you the maximum of answers to use this universal law of attraction, I just ask you this: Play the game!

Remember this! *"There is no magic except the one already in you!"*

<u>Prerequisite:</u>

To come back to the law of attraction, I ask you a contribution for it to work optimally. Everything must be clear in your mind, In order to avoid deviating, you will not be able to concentrate on two aspects of your life, the present one and the one desired, you will have to find the way leading to the detachment, without the daily call to order.

It takes a while, more or less long for the mind to adapt to these new changes that may occur in your life, for some it will take a few weeks, but for others it will take may last for months, depending on the level of anchoring of your current thoughts, and your environment.

It will be necessary before that improve your daily life by small habits to take and stick to it, that's the best for you!

Bear in mind the feeling of prosperity when you have a sword of Damocles on your head will not get you anywhere, debts to pay off, the visit of a usher or others will bring you back to your reality, as well as the attendance of individuals who constantly expose you to their problems and who are in constant negativity, show tact and detachment from them!

They live in a world you do not want anymore, and you do not want someone to destroy all the progress you're going to make, do not be swayed or disassembled by people belittling you, be stronger than that mentally! It's about your life, and it would be a shame to ruin everything because of those who put you on the brakes.

Hope and fear can not cohabit in the same space and at the same frequency. There is always one thought that dominates the other, never both at the same time, and the one that predominates is the reality that you have accepted and that has been part of your life for a long time. So, if you do not want to be afraid of the next day, create the circumstances in this way, so as to have no reason to think about it.

For this, it is necessary to free ourselves from all the hassles of everyday life, it is difficult and will be even more, if the state of mind is not consistent with what we really want.

This is called "having one part of your mind in Paris and the other in Singapore. Thinking about two totally contradictory things, and it's hard to focus on positive thoughts and thinking about your debts and hassle, it will catch up with you all the time if you do not adjust this in the first place, reading this book would not help you in such circumstances.

We all have a role to play, mine is to give you all the possible answers, and the means to implement them concerning the law of attraction.

Yours is to have the spirit "clean", clear, and free from all current problems, I do not know what kind they are and I could not solve them for you, do not confuse me with a magician because you are unconsciously, you are the actor and the spectator of everything that happens to you, but do not think that I will leave you alone, I will explain to you what you must do in the first place.

Understand my point of view! This book is based on two principles: Absolute Trust and Authenticity, and the two are inseparable.

Follow this advice, it is really valuable for the future, and you will thank me later!

In order to be in a calm state of mind, that is to say, without having to look on his bank account if there are some pennies to live, or have the fear of the next day to see a bailiff land for to seize all your furniture, or to imagine a catastrophe to come, I would ask you something really essential:

"To be in harmony with its reality! "

For that, and without delay, solve your current problems, or find solutions or compromises to do it! And above all, keep a very good line of conduct by not trying to put you in difficulties.

For those who do not have work, I recommend you find one and really give you the means to do it!

Some will say to me "yes, it's easy to say! But difficult to apply! ".

If you are having trouble everywhere, including finding a job, then it will be! I'm not here to defeat you or lie to you, but with this type of thoughts, it's clear that you will not find anything, and unfortunately that's part of the law of attraction.

You expressed the deep conviction that everything would be difficult in life, I never claimed the opposite, and I wish for you that you find a job, even if it is not the job of your dreams. There is no shame in being a sweeper or a scavenger, they are ungrateful trades, but you must!

To make a confession, I did a lot of trades at the end of my studies in accounting, it does not mean that I became an accountant or that I got a position with responsibilities, straight out of the cradle because to get positions like this, you need experience, and to get it, you have to prove yourself.

Imagine for a moment! With a bachelor's degree in accounting and training in administrative fields, as an SME-SMI collaborator, to become manager of my own company, also following numerous internships, well, with a lot of luggage, it was not easy for me too.

There were many phases of discouragement, but I had with me a golden father who always lifted me up and who gave me a rebuff, and everyone should have a father like I had, someone fighting, always getting up and raising his entourage, he had that inner strength that I learned to have a little later, after his death in 2011.

During my life, I was a scavenger, sweeper, in the metallurgical industry, I was already unemployed, there were times when I experienced misery, but in my mind, there was this little echo that kept telling me "you can do it! I believe in you ! Have confidence ! You are capable of it! ". This little voice is my inner coach, the one who supports us when everything goes wrong, never neglect it, it is a very precious help.

Try to adopt this state of mind, and you will see! The first results will be felt, even if at the beginning, it's not what you want, you say it's the beginning of the road, and it is not paved with gold, far from it.

Many would not envy the situations that I knew, live in a room of 10m ² without water, nor electricity, in unhygienic conditions and with problems of neighborhood, I know full that envy me of my current life, it was a long, hard road to go, but I did it, and also understand how proud it is, to say "wow," I did not believe it myself!

There are many examples like these, especially from other authors, like Franck Nicolas or Max Piccinini, they know very well where they come from and also know they will not return!

So, do not despair! What has been within my reach, or those of other people, this can also be yours! Barriers do not exist, it is only you who put them, and I will explain it at length in this book.

To get back to work and go back a bit on my words, for those who do not, try to find one, would not it be time to solve your problems and find another better for you !

At this, I give you a little tip to write your resumes, I have already applied in the professional career with a very good response rate:

The parrot technique

This is to read the ads closest to our skills and post them on your resume in bold and bold.

You have to put yourself in the shoes of employers who receive thousands of letters of application, most of them do not even bother to read them because often very busy and usually the letters end up feeding their trash. Why ? They just do not want to strain their eyes at reading fine print, having experienced their eyes reading other letters, if yours is at the end of the pile, that will not be luck for you, and they will not bother!

On the other hand, if you analyze their expectations, for example, if one of them asks for a storekeeper with a CACES 3 and 10 years of experience, then post it on your Curriculum Vitae on the header of this way.

Only use "italian" size envelopes (top opening)

Note in the header for example:

Curriculum Vitae

Warehouse operator
CACES 3
10 years of experience

That's the essence of what they want to know, if their expectations match what you're proposing to them, maybe they'll put your Curriculum Vitae in the backlog of mail waiting, and they'll read it the next day, but the key is to capture the attention.

Also, if you do not have 10 years of experience, there is a parade.

Suppose you only have 8 years of experience, just write this this way.

+ 8 years of experience

The "+" will affect the psychology of the employer and he will say that it is relatively close to his expectations.

Second thing too, and if you have no experience at all, do not hesitate to send resumes, twice, three times, or ten times in a row for two reasons.

Reduce the chances of your candidacy in the trash, there will be a one in ten chance that one of them holds the attention of an employer, but be careful! Leave a period of at least a week, the time required for it to answer you! This does not mean that you have to dwell on only one employer, during the week, nothing prevents you from contacting others by the same process.

There are employers who like motivated people, with or without experience, they admire the involvement in their business, it is true that the diplomas help as well as the experience, but what they admire even more, it is the motivated people. In relation to this, another candidate may have all the necessary diplomas and experience, but if there is no involvement and he is limp, he will not fizzle, and employers want people remaining.

In terms of debt, after you get your first job, start with the most important thing, that is, rent, water and electricity, that's the base.

Then, the other debts starting with the smaller ones, in order to free your mind and be more focused on the following ones! The more you solve your problems, the more you will feel better, clear in your mind.

And if you do not think about it anymore, keep a monthly budget, tighten your belt for a while, the situation will only be temporary, but it's worth it, you have to do violence to get the best, and that's what I have done. Do not be pleased for a few months, and focus your priorities on repayments, follow a very good line of conduct, and life will make you a hundredfold, especially for what will follow inside this book.

Do you wonder the connection between what I just wrote and the law of attraction?

I repeat :

To be in harmony with his reality

It is impossible to have positive thoughts at the same time, if you have negative thoughts making them real everyday, difficult to project yourself into a prosperous state of mind with ideas related to your current problems.

I ask you a lot, I know, but it's really very important, you can not attract to you everything you want if you maintain all that you do not want and that brings you tirelessly to reality, we do not can be aware of success if everything around us shows the opposite.

Rule number 1 so that the law of attraction really works:

HAVE A STATE OF CLEAN SPIRIT

You see ? Just on these first lines, the 12 € that you have dedicated to this book are already well invested, as far as it serves you! And I ask nothing more, except a thank you for these tips, which would be welcome.

My book, which I have put time and energy to write, must be effective, and all the answers on the subject will be there, provided to apply the recommendations to the letter, j I wanted to make it powerful, and it is.

Last but not least, take care of your home, that's where you spend most of your time, and care about your dating.

I believe that everything is said, now, I leave you with your reading, and on these last lines of this chapter, I wish you all, to succeed all that you will undertake!

There will be no limit to what you want, you will discover much more than the everyday can bring you, you will discover what is "above the line"

Wherever you are and whoever you are, I send you my best thoughts, and I will be with you wholeheartedly in all that you do!

Yours truly!
Yoann MERITZA

CHAPTER 2 :
THE MANUAL OF THE MIND

"The secret of change is to focus your energy to create something new, not to fight against the old. "
(Dan Millman)

If there is one word that I would like you to re-member throughout this book, it is "percep-tion". Bob Proctor, another personal develop-ment writer uses the word "attitude," but some-how, the two are related, you'll soon under-stand why.

Many have asked me questions, and some have shown great interest in the subject, and others, a form of impatience.

Does the secret really exist? Nothing to do with Rhonda Byrns' book "The Secret," the subject is so vast that it couldn't fit into one book, and yet, that's what I'm going to try to do, though, I I have already written two on the same theme .

This secret exists, it involves rules that we use unconsciously every day, leading us to either success or failure.

It is a force of attraction that exists around us and in us, but very few know how to use it, even if strangely, they manage to apply it without being aware of it, because of their paradigm. I will explain this last term a little further.

However, I have received some criticism due to the skepticism of some and who do not want to *"waste their time with such nonsense"*
(to use the words of a
 commentator).

And yet, I would say this in this form:

"Assuming it works, why do not you try? "

Everyone was free of his beliefs, and I, having mine as an author, a few years ago, I was not convinced, really not at all, my life was spinning in a vacuum before I saw these wonderful changes that have occurred in my life, and when that happens we can only believe it.

My books are all pieces of the same puzzle, because I can not reveal you all of a sudden, it requires a broad understanding of the subject that a book would not have enough.

To go back a bit, on my book "Guaranteed success", I had evoked two meetings, those with a lady at the casino of Chamonix and the other, with my destiny. Some people on the scene can testify.onnes sur les lieux pourront en témoigner.

To give you more details, what she had written down on a piece of paper, would you like to know what was on it?

I did not talk about it before, because I did not know if it was very interesting on my first book, but to be honest, there was a message to send, a phone number and a name.

From then on, a year had passed since this meeting, we were in January 2018, shortly after New Year's Day, I put my suit in my closet, and I fell back on these notes. They had stayed in one of my jacket pockets, waiting for me to read them, because I did not have a keen interest, not taking this seriously, and what's more, phoning a stranger, it's not Too my kind.

That said, something still pushed me to call this person, although I do not like to disturb, but after a fortnight, I thought *"oh! And then damn! At worst, the person on the phone is hanging in my face, what can I risk more? "*

So, I called! The phone rang for several minutes before the caller picked up his handset.

In a feverish voice, she replied:

i- "Yes allo! Who is speaking ? "

I replied:

y - "Good evening, excuse me for disturbing you, I am Mr MERITZA"

i - What is the purpose of your call?

Not knowing how to formulate, at the same time, difficult to speak to this stranger, I went straight to the point.

Y - "Well, I'm calling, because someone you know probably, Ms. L, gave me your phone number and told me that you could help me."

i - "And how can I help you? "

With these words, I revealed to him my intentions, as well as the message on the piece of paper.

At that moment, he said to me rather harshly:

i- « Mrs. L. told me about you! But still, you have been slow to respond to his request, and I do not have anything to do!"

The discussion was long, and I explained to him why I was late in responding, but finally, we had agreed to a meeting the following week.

And he added before hanging up:

i- "I'm counting on you! Do not let me down!
See you next week ! "

The following week, I had trouble finding the
address, the houses were all alike,
a lot of questions ruminated in my head *(what*
if it was a joke, and if I had gone all this way
for nothing, what will he think of me if I arrive
late?). But after some information, I was at his
door. It opened, and behind, there was an old
man who invited me to return. He had a big
smile and did not tell me that I was late.

His house was filled with old furniture, but I
could not really give a year to these, I only
know they were old. There was no TV, but this
man had a large library, it gave the impression
of coming from another time, far from all modern equipment, but still, the place was welcom-
ing. He invited me to sit on one of those old
armchairs covered with a blanket.

The discussion was long, and he was delighted
to have a visit. It is true that the place was isolated. He offered me the coffee, and he returned to the object of my visit.

He was very familiar with the woman who met me at the casino in Chamonix, also revealing that it was a person often on the move and that there is very little chance of seeing her again.

But, however, he rose from his chair and went to a closet, the doors creaked as he opened it, and he took a notebook from inside it.

He also told me that everything I see, very few people know him, and he would like me to share what I will discover with other people.

My curiosity was stoked, and I can not help but ask him this question:

y - Why me? In what way can I bring something to the greatest number?

He answered me the following thing:

"Inside, there is more than just a secret to discover, and it is not to put in all hands! "

So he gave me this notebook, not knowing how to go about sharing what I was going to discover.

This notebook was a very old manuscript, a kind of diary entitled "the manual of the mind", just the title, I found it odd, but inside, I'll find out later, and you'll know it in this It was more than just a manual.

As I flipped through the notebook, he asked me the following question:

i « - "What are you doing in the life young man? "

y: "- I work in the industry as an operator! "

i "And you do not expect to do anything better? Do you have projects? "

Y "I had it, but with time, I resigned myself! "

i "Yet you are totally unaware of what you are capable of! The problem is not outside, but inside, you have to look inside! "

It puzzled me a bit at first, but as I continued reading, I quickly understood what he meant by that.

There was also an old photo that served as a bookmark, behind it there was an inscription: *"Ed. J. Carly - 1934"*, at least that's what it seemed to be noted, the ink had rubbed off on the cover of the notebook. In the photo, there was a man in his office, standing with his hands on the table, smiling, and surrounded by people, I do not know if it was his family members or the staff of one of them. company, nothing was specified, I do not even know on what occasion it was taken.

To return to this diary, it was written for a very specific purpose, to be shared. It was all part of a process that should never be interrupted.

Since then, I have engaged in a process that I must respect, that's why I started to write books, the conditions were very precise and it is my contribution that would bring me the most in life in the opposite direction, I risk losing everything, and it will be impossible for me to backtrack.

My role is to reveal the secret to the greatest number, as did those who preceded me, and I can not depart from the rule, it is the ultimate condition to lead me to Success, hence the title of my first book.

You will discover the contents of this note-book, here, in these pages, and if I can advise you one thing, once you have succeeded in life, to "pass the relay", and no matter how you will do it , I'm just asking you to do it. Like me, you will understand very quickly why.

This book is an adaptation of the texts from the notebook, it does not correspond with the time when it was written, but reproduces as faithfully as possible its content.

The texts have just been adapted to the news, but the purpose remains the same, what I will tell you is a fabulous story, and it is yours, you will become one of the actors of this book that I feel pretty powerful.

I let you discover the contents of this note-book! Happy reading !

CHAPTER 3:
THE MATRIX

"The new evolutionary and progressive paradigm is to change the collective consciousness to move it forward. "
(Daniel Vallat)

Everyone is the actor of his own life.

If your life would have been different, would you like it?

Your life is like a book of which you are the only author, with an initial situation, a disruptive element (not that which one believes), adventures, a balancing situation and a final situation.

If there is a beginning to everything, we must return to the origins of our being, in order to understand who we are, and why we perceive the world in a certain way.

At the beginning of all existence, there is a birth, yours or mine, virgin of all external information. Our brain, at birth, is empty, it perceives the sound and a little later, the images.

Paradigm

Do you know what this is ? This is the primary information we all acquired from birth.

This information gives us beliefs, good or bad, an analysis of the outside world that will give us a perception of all that we will live thereafter.

We are all programmed in a very specific way to success or failure, and as we grow, we reinforce these beliefs and the perception we have of life.

This paradigm is the matrix of our destiny, it is made thanks to or because of our environment. It is a set of positive or negative beliefs whose roots come from what we call primary information.

The primary coding of this "paradigm" already existed in the belly of your mother, because at that time you were one with the one that carried you. It operated according to a frequency it shared with you, in the same vibratory field. We get emotional programming due to this environment.

Therefore, occupying the same space, we vibrate at the same frequency, and this during the nine months until birth. Clearly, if we inherit the same traits that our parents, namely, the same physical traits of our father or our mother, the frame of our paradigm is included.

From our first day, there is a neuro-associativity between the already well-anchored emotions and the primary information, all that we learn is assimilated to joy, fear, disgust or pleasure, and during the first years of our life, until around the age of 5 to 7, since not everyone is changing at the same pace, these primary beliefs are transformed or consolidated over time.

Subsequently, when we were able to walk, we all made mistakes, and our parents corrected us, unconsciously creating this feeling of fear, always by the neuro-associability, the junction is made between act and consequence, making grow the seed inside your febrile mind of all forms of feelings.

Paradoxically, our primary beliefs are born of our emotions, neuro-associative stimuli are made up of new beliefs, they have both matured and another form.

Shortly after, we continue to grow with the beliefs once fixed in the mind, we have unconsciously created our own vibratory field acting at higher or lower frequencies according to the established beliefs.

These frequencies act on our organism and our environment, they are either positive or negative, attached to our paradigm that serves as a beacon, connected to an umbilical cord form between birth and our present or future actions.

On the assumption that we are hardened over time, it suffices to be shocked emotionally, because of an accident or other circumstances, to bring back what we thought disappeared in us. These emotions have a matrix form, woven of all your beliefs, from your paradigm, and this form evolves with time, but the roots are the same.

Alarm signals still exist when we decide to change direction in life, which makes us doubt our abilities, because of emotions still active, fear of judgment or failure are mainly anchored.

We can follow various methods proposed in personal development, try to change direction, but if we do not change our paradigm, it is almost impossible to change direction, everything will be reduced to permanent failures.

The manual of the mind begins with this part, because it is the origin, and it is the most important, finally, I guess the author wanted to emphasize this point and I understand very clearly its logic . It is interesting to take the problem from the beginning, to give oneself the means to put oneself in psychological conditions, in order to draw to his advantage, and not the opposite, the laws of the universe.

Everything that happens in our life is due to this series of sad or happy events, it would require to change the whole perception that we had throughout our lives, it is a huge job to do on yourself, and I want you to understand this if you want to see things improve in your daily life, no longer be a loser, but a winner.

That said, it is possible to modify this coding, by a process that I would call "detachment". We will see this a little later.

You have accumulated so much negative information about yourself that made the person you are now, and to stay in the same pattern, the more years go by, and the more it will grow in the same direction.

It will be difficult to stop this mechanism on its way, unless you change course, to get to a better destination.

There are beliefs that have led you to believe that you have to be wary of some people, to hate those who have succeeded in life, through those around you who have been for you a school of life (theirs of course)

The information we got was that you had to like or hate this or that individual, that acting in a certain way was good or bad.

To summarize, the life you live is not yours, there is no free will, but a repetition of the situations that existed before, from your parents who did not have the chance of hope, by your friends and relationships from an early age.

Accidents of life that have caused phobias of all kinds, and whose source you do not know.

For example, people with fear of cats or spiders, because they were stung or scratched being small.

This is more difficult to treat, especially if it is part of the paradigm, if the information is negative, there will be so-called "primary" neuro association.

If the matrix of your life was a color, it would be red or blue. One representing fear, and the other, trust. The information you will have later, if it is yellow, it will be interpreted as the green or orange color, creating a feeling affiliated with that same matrix.

This feeling is reinforced by the beliefs of others who taught you their truths. You are very precisely in a collective environment filled with individuals living an experience similar to yours.

It seems that there are two worlds, the one in which you live, filled with modest people who will only teach you what they know about their reality, and then the other, the one you criticize without you having the less free will on the issue.

The Snowman

When I was younger, like all children, at least those who knew the snow, we made snowmen.

At first, it looks like a tiny snowball in the

palm of your hand, whether it's compact or not.

If I had only powder not compacted, we suspect that the effect will be zero, impossible to even roll on the snow.

On the other hand, by consolidating and forming a more compact ball, by rolling it on the snow, it will grow by the effect of accumulation.

Take an example of what I have just mentioned, snow is your life, consolidating it, we can move it forward.

If on the way, there are pebbles or others, the big mass intended to make the body will be filled with these same pebbles or others.

You are half the body of the snowman, and all there is in it is the negative information that can be accumulated there.

If at the beginning your beliefs are that you are dead, that you will come to nothing, and that you must be wary of certain individuals, be afraid of cats or hate the successful people, your convictions thus acquired will have an impact on the rest of your life.

They made fun of you as soon as you spoke, or you had no affinity with the girls in your school, and they also made fun of you, it locked you in your shell, making you shy , and creating difficult situations related to this.

You may not remember it, but if you are in this situation, it is because, somewhere, bad information has remained in you. This has destroyed both your affective and professional relationships, since, if you have as a project to become a salesman with fear in your stomach, to dominate instead of being dominated, and without speaking talent because you have underestimated compared to others. It's a whole set of those little things that make up the person you are right now.

You will ask me "how? "

It's very simple (well, I say that for the way I'm going to explain it to you)

Take something to write, a paper and a pencil, and write down all aspects of your present life in relation to the outside world, if people consider you in a certain way, you do not have a lot of money, your professional and romantic relationships are difficult, and at the same time, in your mind, you think of all these external aspects and ask yourself "why? "

Do not blame the outside world, it's just a reflection of who you are look for the reason why they act this way with you.

It's about knowing the reasons that push them to be unsympathetic or sympathetic with you.

Example:

You have trouble finding love
Why ?
Because you do not dare!
Why ?
Because you are shy!

Why ?

Because the girls in your schools were bad with you when you were young

Why ?

You did not know how to approach them.

Why ?

Because you have not learned!

Why ?

Because no one has shown it to you!

Why ?

Because you did not dare to learn for yourself!

Why ?

Your senses were oriented towards a negative vision of these girls, the first time you had seen one!

Why ?

Your mother or sister gave you a bad picture of them from the first day of your life!

You see ? We come down to the source of the problem that constitutes your current difficulties, the origin of the "why" your romantic or professional relationships are difficult, come from your beliefs from the paradigm.

That said, you are not directly responsible for your actions or beliefs that you have accumulated throughout your life, coming from one place, the "paradigm."

For that, we need to change our internal tag, create another one, and from that point on, create new connections in our mind, redefine the neuro-associativities. We have to remember one thing, every event in our life helps us to move forward, we have to take full advantage of it.

I give you one of the most powerful keys in the universe!

"Stop feeling inferior to others! "

How should you be? Because of the studies they did? Size or physical strength?

We are all part of the same society where there are strong and weak, each having a role to play in this world. But why the heck do not you deserve to enter the camp of the forts? You are exactly the same as everyone you encounter in your daily life, that is, two arms, two legs and one head, you bleed when you cut, just like them, but what is there A great thing about our universe is that our body gives us a power, that of interaction.

The only thing that changes is the frequency that you emit compared to others! Said like that, it's still not clear enough, but rest assured, I'll explain!

If for example, you want to start a business, and you lack self-esteem, it will end with a fiasco (I've been there!), Why?

Since you came into the world, there has always been someone above you, be it parents, school teachers, or business leaders, you've been taught values, some of which are unfounded, making you dependent on a system.

Then, throughout your life, and there I speak bluntly, **you bowed your back** and did odd jobs right to left, with bosses or bosses who belittled you, putting you back in your place as soon as you wanted raise the tone (am I in the right?), in short, no evolution.

It is difficult for you to get angry with a supervisor, because you are deep in your consciousness of his superiority, "How dare you miserable bugger? One of them would say, and as a result, you vibrate at a lower frequency than him, if inside you, you feel less than another, it is clear that you will not evolve!

ENHANCE THE ESTIMATE OF YOUR-SELF!

Some will say, "Yes, I'm proud of myself! "But that's not what I want to talk about, we can be proud of ourselves or others, without feeling underestimated by a narcissistic or other individual.

Since when you raise your voice and realize that you have a superior in front of you, why do not you try the opposite? That is to say, try to maintain good relations, saying "yes, chief! But this time, you will feel above him, feel superior to him, and I can assure you that it will be felt, and I can develop further.

Take a pan of water and pour oil into it, what do you see? Circles of oils, there are big, medium and small.

What you see there is the place of everyone in the universe, there are stronger ones, and others weaker, each vibrating at a different frequency. Human society is built like that, there are sweepers, engineers, bosses, presidents, etc.

Where is your place in there? Do you feel (what you feel) stronger than some and weaker than others?

As long as you maintain that feeling of being inferior to a business leader, you will never become it, or you will try the experiment and you will break your face after a few months, or at best, you will hold a year before to be overwhelmed by debts.

The universe sends you the following message: "You are not made to do anything other than what you are meant for! ", That is, in relation to the relationships you have with others.

I invite you now to feel superior, without you showing it, do what you have to do on a daily basis, and you will see the relationships that will change, no longer be a submissive!

The more your vibration increases, and the more your life will change, only by feeling your surroundings differently!

When you have gained enough confidence, it will increase self-esteem.

If you do not do this first, whatever you do, it will fail.

As far as your relationship with money is concerned, you must first respect your expenses and no longer seek trouble as I said at the beginning, but that's not all!

Take the example of drops of oil in the pan, there are small spheres and larger ones.

Try to put a piece of € 2 on a drop of oil with a diameter of a piece of € 0.10, it will not fit! But the opposite will be possible, we could put two pieces of 0.10 € in a diameter of 2 €. Do you understand better?

Take the test, for my part, I know it works! Condition your mind to be superior to a leader mentally (this must remain in your heart of hearts), and also to other people around you, feel this superiority, keep this for you! Erase this ounce of doubt from your mind, it's very important, and always keep in mind this human superiority! Will you be a winner in these conditions? Without a shadow of a doubt!

If this is not the case, you have to convince yourself better than that, because you are still prey to what I call "hidden doubt" or "latent thinking".

But as everything in the universe has a period of gestation, everything should happen in due time! If it does not work the first time, changes in your environment will make you feel the right moment, on average, I would say it takes between 30 and 90 days to see the first transformations.

Do not forget this, you are the author of what happens to you in your life! And all that is around you is only the reflection of your inner world, what will happen, you will meet new people with a little more important than those that you usually meet! And these will be the representation of yourself! It's magic, is not it?

I would add this, and other authors on the subject will join me on this point, read a lot! Educate yourself! Culture will help you gain confidence and you will not hesitate to talk to people you think are better educated.

One more thing (I told you, the subject is vast!), Respect your entourage just as you would like to be! If, for example, you do not like your boss, it's as if you do not love yourself, it's the mirror theory, each is the reflection of another.

Be sure to treat the outside elements well, because it is your world, when you think bad of your boss for example, and you say that it is a hangman, unconsciously, it will be with you, and more you will maintain this, and so long it will remain so! Never forget that you have enormous creative power, thanks to your spirit, and all the external conditions, it is you who materialize them! The embittered concierge, the baker who makes you charred bread, the lack of luck, the filled parking spaces, finally, everything comes from one place, it comes from you, the only creator of your reality. Try to reconsider your life, to see it differently, and it will be different.

CHAPTER 4:
OVERVIEW

*"Man is the universe in miniature. Man and the world are interdependent. Man is the guarantor of the balance of creation. "
(Amadou Hampâté Bâ)*

Here is a little inspiring story:

As a senior couple living in the south west of France was preparing to travel to Burgundy, their little son was getting married in a few days, and they had to pack their bags.

They used to get up very early, and at the same time, the enthusiasm was very great, because it had been a long time since they had not seen him and their daughter.

After a good night's sleep, it was 5:00 in the morning, everyone was still sleeping in the residence, they took their bags, came out of their house, and loaded them in the trunk.

The car starts, and begins to walk the road that separates them from their destination, everything goes well during the trip, so they decide to take a break on a highway area to eat a piece.

But enthusiasm soon turns into panic, the woman had forgotten her handbag at home, and they were already more than 200 km from home.

Then the husband asked her if she had not put it in the trunk.

She replied:

"No, I assure you, he was hanging on a nail at the entrance"

the husband grumbled:

"- you could not pay attention? "

And the woman replied in the same tone:

"You could have made me think! "

The atmosphere had become electric, there was a flood of reproaches on the part of both, each camping on its positions. And the more they answered, the more intense the argument became, so that the husband lost his vigilance and both had an accident, the car having entered a tree.

The law of attraction is exactly like this old couple, everything we send to the universe comes back to us with the same intensity. And like all disputes, if one or the other does not try to calm the game, it can very quickly degenerate.

The law of attraction is one of the laws of the universe, and it is useful to know them well, because even if it has a great power, the other laws are not to neglect to attract to you everything you desire.

The frequencies of the universe

Who is the universe? The answer is simple, it's about yourself, or at least you're part of it, the piece of a very big puzzle that vibrates at a certain frequency with other elements of this set.

To explain you the frequencies they exist in two forms, positive waves and negative waves. And depending on their intensity, what we hope or fear will materialize or not!

During our life, we accumulate a lot of resentment towards life, we reproach a lot of things with all around us, but what we know less is that everything we experience resonates like a message to the universe, but finally, who knows what the universe represents?

He is all around us and in us, and whether it is through words or emotions, we send him messages in the form of frequencies.

The interactions of your inner and outer world are a manifestation of these frequencies, they vibrate in harmony.

You are calibrated on the same frequency as the universe, what I mean by that is that everything you send to it, you will be returned by its material or immaterial equivalent.

You do not feel confident, some will feel it, what you think is not visible, but what you emit is perceptible, it emerges in you an energy that your entourage will benefit (if you lack confidence for example)), or will respect you (if you are confident with yourself and others).

In addition, you will attract to all people working at the same frequency as you.

The laws of the universe operate at higher or lower frequencies, there is a transmitter and a receiver, the inner and outer worlds exchange the same waves, it is the harmonization and react in time and space.

If, for example, you have the dominant feeling of fear associated with the visit of a bailiff, this will happen. On the other hand if you wish to have a prosperous life, but with a very weak enthusiasm by telling you deep down that it will not happen, that's what will happen. To want something, you have to feel the burning desire, that is to say for example, if you like music on your radio, but the sound is very low, you will not appreciate it, turn the volume knob, and the magic will work! A stronger signal amplifies the law of attraction.

Fear and excitement are two opposing feelings that operate at high frequencies at opposite ends of each other. Like the North Pole and the South Pole, there are two extremes.

What prevents the process of materializing desires is also related to lack of emphasis, it is as if, for example, you participate in selection tests to become actors in a play. If you recite your text flatly, as you did in school, without the dominant feeling, connected to the body, if you lack authenticity in what you play and you do not believe it, the jury charged to recruit the good actor will tell you *"go home! "*

What you will have to learn to dominate is your fear of tomorrow, and hope and enthusiasm. Without asking the question of why and how it will happen, always keep an objective in mind and believe strongly in it.

For that, you will have to move cursors, that of the fear down, and that of the enthusiasm up, then, to keep a goal in mind and be excited to know the continuation with a great hope that this will come true, despite the snags of life that will have to be mitigated by seeking solutions rather than worrying.

The tiles in life, it happens, but we must not dramatize or increase their importance, what must be done is to say that all difficulties can be solved and to believe firmly, if you believe with all your heart that this will be solved, then, it will be solved in a way or else, the possibilities of the universe are multiple.

The universe is infinite, and we must not limit ourselves, go beyond, fight for what we want, it is only for you that it is the responsibility of what you really want, and it's up to you too to go get what you want, take everything you need, and act in consequence, do not let yourself be destabilized by external events, which is only the materialization of your inner inner being do you want something from the universe? So do everything in your power to get there! (I'll show you how at the end of the book).

Staying on the same course, without procrastinating or engaging in foolish behavior, you will get it if you have this intimate conviction that it will happen, and by training you to create the enthusiasm you need.

The diagram below shows you technically how the universe works.

The frequencies of the universe

Scheme fear

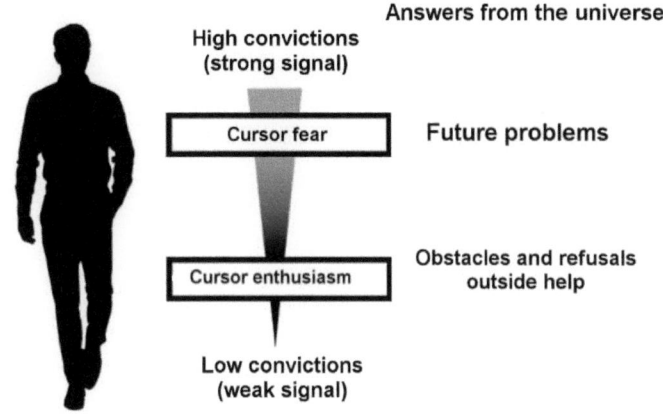

Scheme enthusiasm

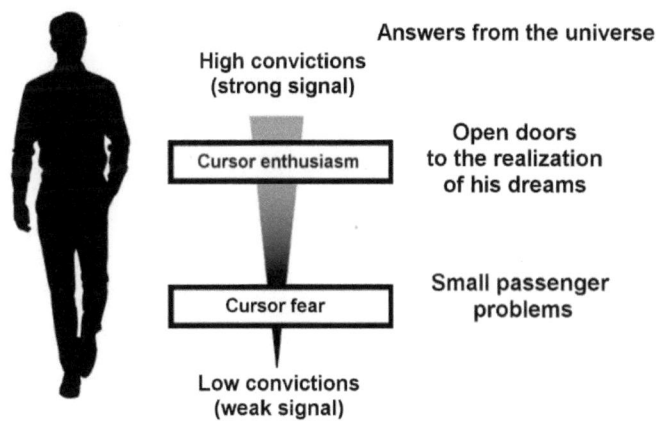

What is enthusiasm?

Or how to experience this feeling? Many have forgotten how to be enthusiastic, resigned to feeling this type of emotion, it seems to be a distant memory.

But remember the last time you waited impatiently for Santa's visit, it goes back a long way in the youth for most of you, and after that, life has gone a long way from dreams and illusions.

I would like you to remember those moments of your life, the hope of receiving a long-desired gift, of feeling your heart beat and of having your head full of dreams to be dazed, for example, I remember waiting a beautiful bike, I always thought about it when I was young, my eyes were full of stars.

Try to remember those moments where you felt that feeling, think of something you want, hopefully that will happen, focus on it, intensify the purpose of your desires and silence the other part of your mind that whispers to you *"no, it will never work!"*.

Silence that thought, gag her, she's talking too much! And cherish this desire every day as if it would happen, without setting a date, just that it will materialize someday.

To make the comparison with the fear that something will happen, this has often happened, so why would not it work with enthusiasm? Think about it!

Enthusiasm, happiness, and love have a strong appealing power, but what blocks you are your old beliefs, in the form of thoughts well hidden deep within you. This tiny doubt is rooted in your mind.

You are the master of your thoughts and your reality, everything that happens around you, you provoke it without really being aware of it, because of a bad perception of the outside world and of your own person.

Learn to see yourself differently and look at the world around you differently, and if you can convince yourself, you'll be in another world, but it will be the same, except that the conditions will have changed.

The mirror theory

The universe is a gigantic mirror that sends us an image, and generally, it's not the one we expect.

If we think too much of ourselves, of our comfort, to believe ourselves superior to others, we will generate a jealous behavior on the part of our friends or relatives..

In fact, we would like to portray someone as altruistic, with selfish behavior, and what happens with the mirror theory, the image that is referred to us is that of selfish people who are say altruists, do you imagine the imposture? Everything around you is built on the same pattern, from head to toe, and up to your fingertips, the image you get is exactly what you are!

If there is a sentence that sums up well what I just mentioned:

The universe is your mirror and you are the mirror of the universe!

In this sentence alone you have an overview of the laws of the universe.

If all that constitutes the universe is personi-fied, time and space would be formed to be nothing but your own reflection in a mirror.

When we criticize a person, it is a part of our universe, it is our own reflection, and that's what we send him who determines who we are, being criticized in our turn.

To illustrate my words, let's take an example:

Put yourself in front of your mirror and watch your reflection! Then, put your finger on the mirror, you will see your finger connect with your reflection.

What you see is a representation of yourself,

you like or hate what you see, it's how you feel inside yourself.

The universe works the same way, it creates a harmony between you and him.

When you have some form of thought, it's as if you're pointing at the mirror, you're connected with it, and you're reflecting the image of that same thought.

If you do not like yourself, you will have a feeling of inner lack of confidence, which will be expressed in the outside world, because everything in this universe is felt.

The universe is only a reflection of our actions and our thoughts.

The balance

Do you know the law of Talion? The universe works according to the same principles:

"Eye for eye, and tooth for tooth! "

Whatever you do or think, the universe works with the principle of balancing events. And as it is written in the Bible:

"Give and you will receive! "

Sow the positive and you will reap the positive, share love, and you will get back, that's how the universe works. By learning to listen to him and accept what he tells you.

Stop thinking negatively!

As I mentioned in my first book, "Success Guaranteed", once you think of a disaster, it will happen if you release attention to it. Thinking about it starts a process in the universe.

When you play squash, for example, you have mastery of the ball, but at when you release your attention, it comes to your face at the same intensity as you sent it. This is called the "return shock" or the "boomerang effect".

The universe is the same as this tennis ball, the more you struggle thinking you can counter the return of it, telling you "I will prevent the event from happening! And the more you'll get tired of firing shots on a concrete wall.

When a process is started, it can not be stopped. It's as if your banker told you *"It's good! We forget your € 10,000 of debt!"* You have to continue paying until you pay off the debt. However, you can pay in installments and find other arrangements out of court, but in any case, nothing can stop the process being completed.

As for the example of the tennis ball, it's all about minimizing the impact that the next shot will have. Gradually reduce it by having healthier thoughts! How? By telling you that this difficulty can be solved, and by giving less importance. Do not let yourself be dominated by feelings of panic, but resonate in terms of solutions, which directs your mind to the positive! Everything can be arranged if we put the forms.

The less importance you attach to having no more "disaster" patterns in your head, trying to solve your problems, the less violent the return, it will soften until you see the contours of the tennis ball. It will gradually lose its intensity and fall back to the ground before you even reach it, and this law is universal.

What you have to do is think in terms of solutions rather than problems, it will trigger another process, that of mitigation, and you will feel more comfortable.

The "cyclics", as mentioned in my first book, respond to this same law, we attract what we think, and if it is not yet entered into your life, what you thought is on the way, but here, what prevents the materialization of your desires is the frequency, the fact of thinking only is not enough, one must create a form of osmosis between what one thinks and the feeling experienced, and the more one gains in intensity, the more likely it is to materialize.

Keep hope that things get better, because it will work out, the universe needs this balance to work.

"Cyclics" are two forms of energy forming vortices, one is positive, the other is negative.

They work through the mind, but the fact that you do not get what you ask for does not mean anything in itself, it is happening, but you do not have enough positive magnetism to speed up the process.

Also, your energy is "charged", that is to say that you had made the habit of resigning yourself. It is your deep nature that charges you with negative energy.

Try to associate the desire to have more money with a very strong positive feeling! Cultivate your enthusiasm! And also I will come back later on a point that can prevent you from materializing what you want, it is about *"latent thinking"*.

Start now to cultivate positive thoughts, and I

give you this sentence to note a piece of paper that you will consult in due course if you forget it: *"today is a good day, the best of all, and tomorrow she will be even better! "*.

Keep this in mind, stop complaining and become more responsible for your actions and thoughts.

Whatever you think is happening, at higher or lower intensity. However, what is holding back the process is the dominant negative thoughts and expectations, which is synonymous with "lack", and you will reap only what you have been thinking about, that is, "the lack "because the frequency of it is stronger.

Charge positively and do not be in the future, live the present moment as if you had got what you want, and repeat the magic sentence quoted above, permeate it in your mind.

Unfortunately, the problems will follow their course, as I said, we can not stop a process already started, let them happen, accept that it happens and tell you that behind it is good news. Things will have to be rebalanced.

The old schema

Now, I'd like you to stop for a moment and look around! What do you see and how do you perceive what is in your environment?

Everything you see, feel, or hear, I may shock you, but you have provoked it, that is, you have attracted the conditions of your present life, and you are unconsciously responsible for it ! How? Because of your limiting beliefs.

Let me explain, there is a certain relationship between you and the world around you, and depending on how you perceive and feel it, what you send to the universe and what you receive is in perfect harmony; for example, if you think you're out of luck in life, you create the conditions that make you never have one!

It's simple ! The universe responds effectively to you, and what you say or think is the fruit of your associated emotions.

And concerning the law of attraction? It works all the time, you are permanently connected to the universe, as well in what you think, what you say, and how you feel, everything is connected.

If you say that you are bad, all the circumstances will make you so, and the more the universe will send you back that conviction and more it will be anchored in you! And rebelote every time.

It is one of the laws of the universe, that of cause and effect.

In order to reverse the trend, I invite you to do the following thing!

Stop complaining ! Because what happens to you are only the conditions that you have issued before, and the more you entertain those thoughts, the more they will come back to you like a boomerang!

Learn to do the opposite, that is to say, instead of complaining, feel gratitude, even if outside events do not lend to it!

A short time ago, I was on the Facebook page of a life coach, and at the sight of some comments, it was for me very informative, not in the beliefs that certain individuals, I summarize in a few lines and you will understand why the law of attraction will not work on them:

- *"it's a stupid thing, it does not work! "*
(the commentator maintains the fact that it does not work!)

- *"how to be sure that it works? "*
(the commentator is doubtful!)

- *"Even when it's simple, it's not always easy! "*
(Actually, the commentator maintains the fact that it is not always easy!)

- *"I never had a chance, why would it change? Must be realistic! "*

(This one has a very down-to-earth design, and maintains his bad luck)

These people are prey to what I call "the schema", they have built an identity about the circumstances of their lives, everything that happens to them is felt as a fatality, and they are right ... they are right .... only, what they are not really aware of is that they build this scheme, maintain it, nourish it, referring to their respective experiences, and this sounds like a message sent to the universe, and if these people do not change course, they continue to feed the universe of negative thoughts, it will send them exactly the same signal.

Now, what is possible to do, is that instead of complaining, they should be grateful! Some will say *"nice! I am grateful because my car is down, my wife left me, and I fell down the stairs!"* Most of you thought about it sarcastically, did not you? (I guess a little!)

And that's why you read me in the hope of finding a cure for all this guigne that pursues you, in this case, I would answer you that you have not yet understood!

All you experience are the outward aspects of what you have created before, and kept alive by your thoughts, and the universe sends it back and forth to you

figure, but still, some do not understand!

You can choose your life! Create it differently! This is your only way out, stop with its old be-liefs from the old scheme! You fall inexorably into the same vicious circle and that poisons your existence!

This simple choice is offered to you! Either you continue to complain and rehash the same things by complaining (and you'll have reason to continue complaining, because the universe will always see you the same), or you change your view of things, to go far beyond your thinking, without recreating the circumstances of your misfortune, having gratitude (even if it may seem absurd and it is your old schema that speaks), and you will reap all that the uni-verse has to offer you !

Have the recognition to be alive, to have a TV, a car, a woman in your life, because for every-one, this is not the case, and you do not have any idea of what to what you can have grati-tude.

Experience this recognition of being alive, who knows what will happen tomorrow, it will depend only on you!

Let the problems of your old schema run out, most of them need some time before they go down, because they are still in progress and must be completed!

The more recognition you have, the more the universe will give you a little more, and the more you complain about your life, and the more circumstances you have in your life will give you reasons to keep doing it!

You are the creator of the circumstances of your reality

everything that you send

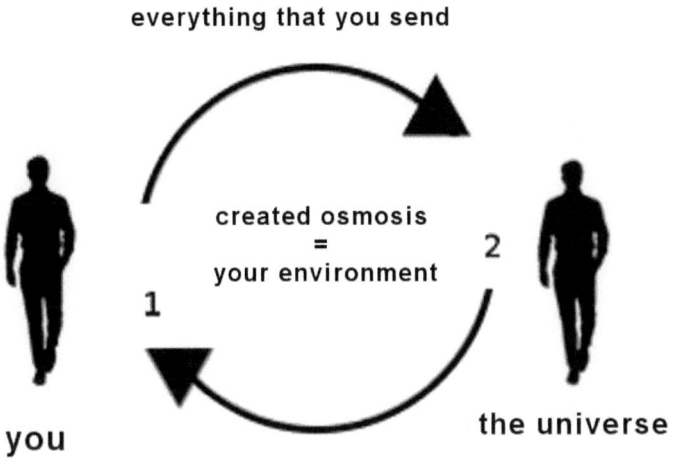

created osmosis
=
your environment

1

2

you

the universe

all that you receive in parallel

1 : What the universe sends you reinforces or preserves your beliefs

2 : reboots the process

See your future with hope and feel that good events will happen!

Do not forget that it is you who causes every-thing that happens to you! When you start a project and it does not work, it's because at the bottom of you, you do not believe it, because you ask yourself too many conditions or limits.

Just look at your destination on the horizon and not when you're going to get there, I understand your eagerness, and I've been there. If something must happen, it will hap-pen! Only, you must be aware that you are prey to your old beliefs, and the life you lead follows its course with its lot of problems, but rest assured! Everything has a term, and re-member this:

The more you will have negative thoughts, in tune with your reality, resigned and fatalistic, and the less it will lose in intensity, involuntar-ily, you reject the maturity of your problems because:

"You see them all the time! "

Would not it be better to look elsewhere with hope and enthusiasm? Of course, there will be hard knocks, but you are still in the infernal spiral, but if you feel that the events will improve, they will improve, just leave the time to "the battery" to unload the negative spiral will lose in intensity, and will result in a transmission of energies from negative to positive.

For this, you must convince yourself tirelessly by reciting this magic phrase every night before going to bed and getting up in the morning:

"Today is a good day, the best of all, and tomorrow it will be better and better! "

Write it down on a piece of paper that you will keep on you! Stop thinking in terms of problems, but solutions, whenever a day goes wrong, do not throw the spotlight on negative events, because I tell you, tomorrow will always be better if you really decide!

THE VIRTUOUS AND VICIOUS CIRCLE

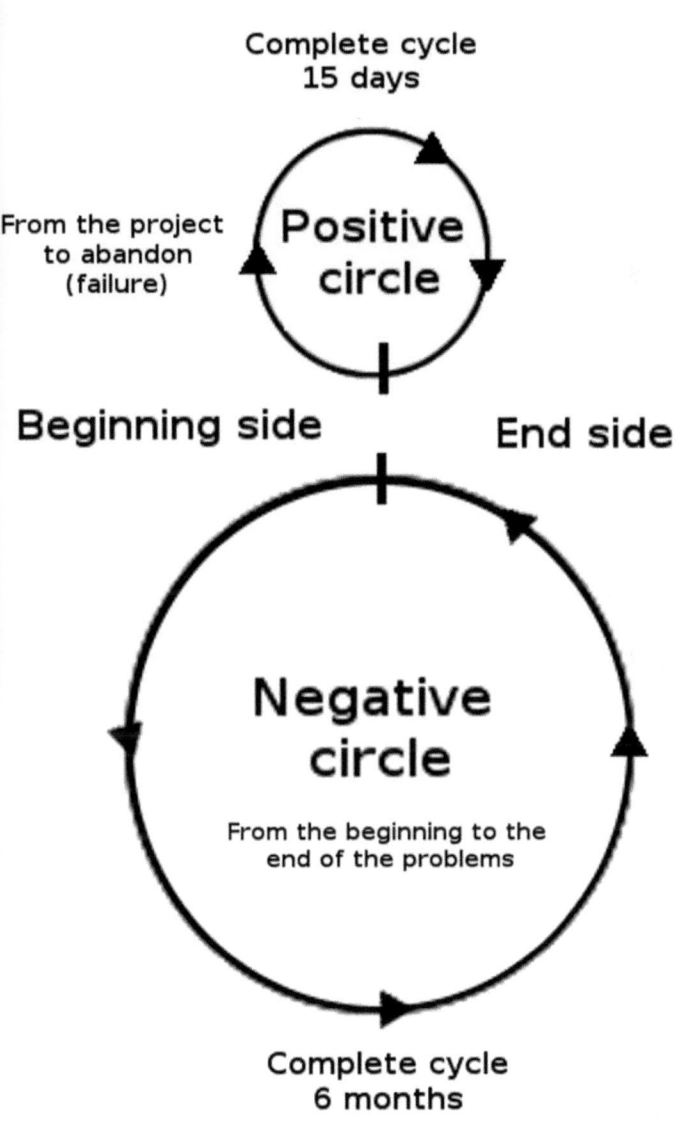

Complete cycle
15 days

From the project
to abandon
(failure)

Positive
circle

Beginning side

End side

Negative
circle

From the beginning to the
end of the problems

Complete cycle
6 months

CHAPTER 5:
THE LAWS OF THE UNIVERSE

"Live with a purpose, and leave the result to the great law of the universe. "
(Zengetsu)

All that constitutes our being and the world around us is the universe.

It acts all around us and through us in the form of positive or negative energies, which, depending on their intensity, attract or repel objects and circumstances like a magnet, they exist both on the material and immaterial level.

There are two worlds that constitute the universe, the one around us, which is the environment in which we evolve, and the inner world, that of our thoughts, it is composed of our beliefs, resulting from the perception that we have, themselves from our neuro-associations between emotions already anchored in us and the incoming information in our mind.

All that constitutes our being and the world around us is the universe.

It acts all around us and through us in the form of positive or negative energies, which, depending on their intensity, attract or repel objects and circumstances like a magnet, they exist both on the material and immaterial level.

There are two worlds that constitute the universe, the one around us, which is the environment in which we evolve, and the inner world, that of our thoughts, it is composed of our beliefs, resulting from the perception that we have, themselves from our neuro-associations between emotions already anchored in us and the incoming information in our mind.

Each individual represents only a fragment of the universe, we are all part of one and the same, vibrating each one at a frequency that attracts us or pushes us back together.

The laws of the universe exist, but very few know how they actually work. It attracts to us all that we think, in order to live with all its benefits.

However, the universe works according to its own rules, and the law of attraction alone can not bring you all that you desire, because there are fourteen main laws, all related to each other.

1 : The law of divine unity

In the universe, everything is connected, both the thoughts, the actions, the objects, the persons or circumstances, relating to this law, we all emanate from the same divine source. We are all part of the same vibrating ensemble at different frequencies. We are both creators and creations, which comes from the outside world is the fruit of our inner world, because we have attracted them to us unconsciously.

2 : The law of vibration

It works by frequencies, everything that travels in the universe has its own energies, functioning or not in harmony. The higher the vibratory frequency, the more it is in osmosis between the desire (or fear) and the universe, in short, we draw to ourselves all that we desire or fear according to the intensity of our thoughts and emotions.

3 : The law of action

All that we desire must be accompanied by an action leading to the desired goal, and that, whatever the size of this one, what is important is the effort and the intensity tested in its direction. Every commitment we make generates a reaction due to this law. Believing or wanting something is not enough! You have to do something towards your goals and not give up.

4 : The law of correspondence

What happens inside of us is what happens on the outside, the outside is similar inside. We are unconsciously the creators of our own reality, everything that happens in your life is the result of your thoughts related to the paradigm. And the more we affirm it because of our limiting beliefs, the more we move in our world in the same direction.

5 : *The law of cause and effect*

It states that nothing happens at random or out-side the universal laws. All actions cause a re-action. To summarize this law, we reap what we sow, voluntarily or not, that is why we must pay attention to what we emit. We are both aware of the reality we are creating, and we are re-engaging the process by believing that everything that happens to us comes only from the outside world.

6 : *The law of compensation*

Everything you give to the universe will come to you in different forms with the same inten-sity, and the more we give, the more we get. These are not just objects of the physical world, gifts can be spiritual.

7 : *The law of attraction*

It is at the center of my book, although the oth-er laws have their utility and are in correspond-ence with each other, we attract to us all that is in agreement with the laws of the universe. It has been functioning continuously since birth, and everything around us is the manifestation of what we thought about.

8 : The law of transmission of energy

It consists of not being trapped in negative thoughts, but on the contrary, to see the positive side of each situation. Your thoughts change your negative frequency and turn into positive frequency depending on the intensity, depending on your level of enthusiasm or anxiety that gives weight to the scales. Do not let yourself be dominated by events! Behind the clouds, there is always the sun, do not give up!

9 : The law of gestation

Before all things come to you in the universe, it takes a period of gestation, like the seed that becomes a plant, or an embryo that becomes a baby, everything in the universe needs a period of adaptation, and he sows circumstances that lead you to the desired end. The gestation law follows a cycle that can not be interrupted and the previous circumstances must continue to occur before any change, this is called "transition phase"

10 : *The law of relativity*

Everything that we send to the universe has a relative answer to the frequency emitted, whether it is good or bad, our thoughts and our words (voluntary or not) trigger a process that must continue until the end.

11 : *The law of polarity*

It states that we all have a contrary. There can be no heat without the cold, there can be no high without the bottom. Just as the vibratory frequencies, for the same emotion, can not be both high and low, it is either one or the other. It is impossible to see our strength if we perceive ourselves as a weak person.

12 : *The law of rhythm*

Everything in the universe works in rhythm, the seconds give minutes, then hours, the day succeeds the night, nothing is static! Everything moves at his own pace.

13 : The law of belief

This law states that everything we believe to be true becomes our reality, but this law does not work if we only think about one thing, we must have the intimate conviction that it will happen. Our limiting beliefs create our reality in which we evolve.

14 : The law of the genre

This law states that everything in the universe has its own characteristics. The masculine differs from the feminine, the good differs from the bad, etc..…

To use the laws of the universe in an optimal way

I will give you the famous secret that I learned a few years ago and give you the keys to success. When you understand what I want to talk about, it will be something very powerful once you have mastered the very essence of what you will learn!

In spite of all that you have read on the subject, you are missing something essential, something very important that goes against your evolution in your environment.

What you have around you is yours, friends, everyday things, your boyfriend, your job and your salary.

You have a car ..... it's good, the accommodation you like ... perfect, you like your work ...... so much better ... .., and you feel that you have everything you need to be happy ..... that's great !

Already, the good news is that you feel good about what you have! There is no debt, no external worries with other people, everything goes well with your partner, as I said at the beginning of the book, you have a stable situation.

But deep inside you, do not you want to see beyond this psychological line that you created yourself? Do not you want to go "above the line"?

Let me explain, what you are currently experiencing is called "your comfort zone", that means that you can be satisfied with what you have, without trying to go further, but is it because you want this situation Do you like it, or do you think it's impossible for you to go beyond?

I remember when I was younger, when I had my first car, I was happy with my little R5. I felt a certain pride in riding with her! It was for me synonymous with independence, but very quickly, I got tired of this car, wanting to have bigger.

Subsequently, I was sold a minivan for a sum that seemed already important to me being young, € 1000, rolling with, I took the importance and height, very proud of this vehicle, my little R5 was became very small, and I wondered "how could I ride with that? ".

But this minivan, someone vandalized me, crushing me the four tires. I did not have the financial means to replace these. So, a neighbor offered me a deal, that of exchanging my mini-van for a 405, a diesel vehicle. I saw the economic side of the vehicle, gasoline being more expensive in 2006, the diesel was less than 1 € per liter and it consumed very little despite its age (it was 1988), I have took advantage of this vehicle, I did miles with it for years, and I still said to myself "how do I could I ride with this vehicle that consumed so much? "

That will make you smile, but this vehicle, I got tired of it, wanting something a little more recent! So, I bought for a little more expensive, an Xsara of 1999 (model which seemed to me a little more recent, and which more is Diesel), at the beginning, I found this super to roll with this car, but thereafter Guess what, I got tired of it ... .. after two years ... .. because it had a fault, its high mileage!

Subsequently, I bought a Zafira, even more expensive (which I thought I was!), And thinking back to my old vehicles, the distant R5 seemed to me little next, one day, I parked next to one of them and to speak harshly, for me, it had become a miserable car, what I felt is a little more important than the time, and curious thing, why do vehicles seem to "shrink"? My perception of my old cars had changed!

A little later, I changed my vehicle, something a little bigger and much more expensive, I bought a Kuga, it was SUV fashion and it meant for me a form of prestige, I let you guess how I perceived my R5, it seemed to be (I ex-aggerate saying this) a child vehicle, so it seemed small next to my large SUV.

All this to tell you that when the conditions of our life change, our perception of things and events changes with it, everything that was thought out of reach and size eventually be-comes smaller.

All that to say that the more one takes height, and the more the perception changes! But here we are, for the most part, we believe to be at the maximum of our capacity and we are satis-fied with what we have, we estimate not to cross the line above.

What's missing in your mind is this little step above, it's going beyond your limiting beliefs that deprives you of the life you deserve, and despite all that I've said d other in this book, what you miss ... .. is to have…

…. THE MIND ABOVE THE LINE.

To describe this in more detail, how do you perceive yourself and how do you see the world around you? Do you feel good about what you live on a daily basis?

Of course, you have no problem, everything is fine and some by, that's good, but ... where are your dreams? Have you become so resigned as to be content with the crumbs of life? Your mind has been conditioned in this way, creating that deep conviction that you can not do anything else.

The message that you send to the universe is as you receive it, the external circumstances are the ones you have created unconsciously, and trapped in your beliefs ... ... you think you no longer have magic deep inside you, like when you were a child

There are three circumstances in your evolution that have driven you to some form of perception:

Through your education, be it parental, school, or professional, there has been someone above you all your life, and it has become unconsciously a habit for you, both in the feeling and in the perception, even if you have the will to exceed you, if you continue having this type of perception, you will not go anywhere, what is necessary, it is to put oneself at the level of those which you believe superior, it is to change the angle of view, with your mind, you will go up a notch and no longer perceive a superior as someone imposing, but as someone like you, such that you will see a friend, try to put yourself in his place and analyze his point of view, for him, you are like the R5 mentioned a little higher.

From your surroundings, whether it is your family or your acquaintances, without saying "friends" with their precious advice without having tried anything in their life, but you have listened to these people with your child-ish naivety, knowing false beliefs , such as you were no, unable to do some things everyday, suddenly they were the ones who became more imposing, even though they took an un-conscious pleasure to feel important to you, and that you has followed your whole life, even if you think the opposite, it is your inter-nal perception in relation to the outside world, so that this type of thoughts has been inter-cepted by the universe that has answered you to the effective to align yourself, to be in os-mosis with the circumstances that led you to believe that you were a loser, you perceive yourself as such, because of what you have sent to the universe, and because of what he has re sent into your environment, forming a cause-and-effect pattern and so on.

By the value given to your environment, when you were in school, or even through parenting education, depending on where you came from, you were taught some beliefs and the value of things, to associate the value to objects, from the least important to the most important, so that the amounts that seem imposing to you are inaccessible, and that you will not be able to offer you a dream life with a house, a sports car or even make trips on paradise islands, and what is most heartbreaking is that television reminds you every time, with princely weddings and luxury, which gives you a dream, and the inner desire of to be a day like them, but it will not be possible because "you do not have the financial means".

In your microcosm, there are people above you and below, and you stand between the two (you guessed it even without marking it), you were told what shape society had, what Square had each of us to make this little world work. And as I explained above, the universe sends you the message, "You will not go higher than you are destined to do," and the external circumstances make you believe it, so much so that you consolidate the message of the universe, which consolidates in turn, and again, and again, and again ......

The commonality between the education you have had, the beliefs you have been given by those around you, and the value you have been given to things in your environment all have one thing in common:

THAT "SEEMS" ABOVE TO YOU!

Think carefully about how you perceive yourself! And here I come back to the law of polarity, there is always a plus, and a minus, a positive side and the other negative, where is your environment? And where are you?

Everything seems superior to you, as imposing as a mountain like Mont Blanc, for a novice mountaineer, he comes to this mountain and finds this imposing, so he climbs and he climbs, and more what he seemed insurmountable it is less! Then, he starts again and perceives the mountain differently, a little more relaxed, he arrives there with a little more ease than the first time. He is gaining confidence!

But if he climbs the K2, everything that seemed huge becomes smaller in his perception, and Mont Blanc seems tiny next.

Look around you!

- A house seems more expensive!
- A mountain seems higher!
- People seem to have more luck than you!
- A millionaire has more money than you!
- A boss has more authority than you!

What you perceive is that others always have "more," so I'll let you guess where you are, in the "less"! and unconsciously, you feel devalued, diminished, and that is why the law of attraction can not work on you until you take a little more height with your mind, realign yourself with all the aspects of your life that you consider to be superior.

With a little common sense, you want to feel like a millionaire, but on the other hand, you perceive the millionaire superior to you, so, you are inferior, for a business leader, it's the same, and others circumstances also, and that comes from one place, the way you perceive your outer world.

Here lies all the trick of the law of attraction, and for it to work 100%, you have to feel superior (and not believe yourself superior), perceive a rich person as your equal, like a friend (you you do not have to be real, but who knows?)

To help you, I'll give you an exercise to do, and I hear another one who shouts *"one more?"* And I would say that you do not have to try them all at the same time, test in one or two, and you will see the events changing around you, because everything I have already mentioned works!

In an isolated place, you will stand with your feet together and your arms body ! Close your eyes, then breathe normally!

You will act as if energy from the ground goes up from head to foot, and you will feel as if you are growing inside!

Put your hands palms up at the waist, and you will go back slowly, as if you wanted to help this energy to go through your body! Made as if several waves crossed you and went up to the head!

In your mind, imagine someone who seems to you superior, and you go at the same time as you put your energy up, reduce that person to the appearance of a child or a small person, and you will you feel superior to her!

Do this for 10 or 20 minutes a day, several sessions can help you raise self-esteem, and if you do it right, the next time you see this person, it will look different!

You can try with a mountain, or a bag of money, the result will be the same, you will not have the same perception as before!

I tell you, it really works! And there is nothing magic about it, it is you who initiate the process of change. And I can congratulate you now, because you have reached a new level! That of insurance in yourself!

Everything will seem so natural to you that you will not have any more brakes to ask, for example, a loan from a banker if in your mind you program it so that it accepts everything you ask for.

CHAPTER 6:
THE ENVIRONMENT

*"Our thought system destroys our environ-
ment, we would have to change our thoughts
to protect ourselves. "*
(Steve Lambert)

We all live in the same universe with two types
of environments. Everything that's going on
around us is exactly the same, the only thing
that varies is the situation analysis.

First there is the one outside the carnal enve-
lope, common to all mortals, which is static, it
is exactly the same thing, the air that we
breathe, the grass that the we crowd or the
water we drink, everything is the same.

Then there is the one inside our body, which is
the vehicle that allows us to interact with the
outside world, the environment is dynamic and
can be modified thanks to the unconscious.

Each being in our outer world reacts differently to this one, following their own pattern of life.

That is to say, we are all programmed to feel, through our five senses, the outside world in different ways, according to our points of view.

Perception

What characterizes human nature is its ego, and we all have one, more or less pronounced. What seems rather paradoxical when an individual says he is altruistic, he expects it to be seen as such, but on the contrary, he sends the image of someone who wants to show himself, centered on his person, and usually he ends up alone, because he is interested in nothing but himself.

I remember a few years ago, I saw a picture of a man next to an invalid, he was in a wheelchair. The question that crossed my mind is, what was this person waiting for next to this invalid? Did he want to show his best day or is it a photo without ulterior motives with pure intentions?

Because of this, and if there is one thing to know about the universe, it acts in us and around us. We can not continue to whine or hate others because it sends a bad signal that will affect our lives if we do not change our way of thinking or acting.

What drives an individual to perceive us in a certain way?

Look around you! What do you see ? Always the same people who have a certain lifestyle and behaviors. For you, it is quite difficult to perceive, since you have made the habit of rubbing shoulders with them, but by repeating what I have already mentioned in the preceding lines, the people lacking assertiveness, respect or and who are constantly in criticism or self-criticism are the ones who fare the least in life.

Example :

Poor people criticize the rich or those who are successful when we almost never see the opposite happen. They have thoughts of opulence and prosperity, always upward-spirited, and constantly seeking self-transcendence.

When the conditions of a person change, the entourage changes, whether in behavior towards you, or felt.

The work of the perception of the world must be done on your own, I do not invite you to see some people who have shaped your life, in some cases it would be impossible (living in a far country, or being dead for example).

But to restructure all the events in your head, thinking back to those people who have been harmful to you.

Aspects of perception

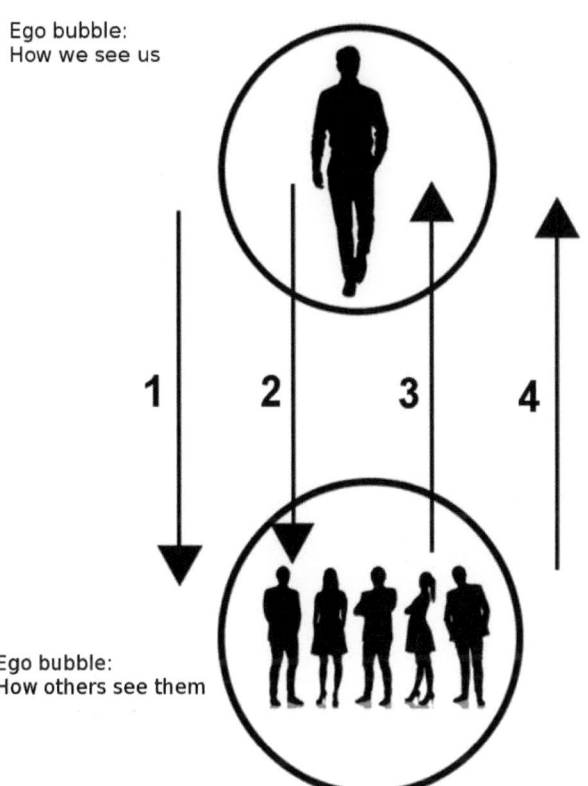

Ego bubble:
How we see us

Ego bubble:
How others see them

1- **How do you perceive others**

2 - **How do you think you are perceived**

3 - **How others think they are perceived**

4 - **How they perceive you**

How to remedy this?

By reconsidering the perception of the world around you.

This will avoid attracting to you everything you do not want or more. Take a step back and stop feeling weak in front of the individuals who are, I remind you, only the reflection of what you are!

The way you think will affect your environment, but beware, it's not just about thinking, it would be too easy otherwise! There are many things to take into account

Apart from the fact that most who have money or success or that their relations are at best, and yet you are in all respects identical (it surprises you?)

The only thing that differentiates you from them is the perception of the world around them, and the esteem they have about it, of how they feel about others. Everything is related to this perception.

What is your value?

I do not ask you to give me an amount you will understand! But in the eyes of everyone you have or will have in your life, what are you worth?

There is a distinction between the value we give ourselves and the value that those around us give us. And in the depths of you lies that little voice that whispers to you that if you believe it, you will get there. ! However, to go back a bit, your beliefs come from the neuro-associativity between the paradigm and the incoming information.

Your beliefs come from your childhood, but they have been reinforced over time. Anything you have been taught about yourself that was unfounded, saying that you were nil or unable to do certain things, causing a drop in self-esteem. But if your entourage had taken into account your emotions, he would have encouraged you, giving you greater value, and you would have felt this deep inside you.

You, being curious about everything, were awake in front of the world that still surrounds you today, experiencing enthusiasm, anger, but also fear, every little thing that your entourage has transmitted to you has had its lot of meanings for good or bad.

Your parents prevented you from touching certain everyday objects, and created at the same time a feeling related to this prohibition, by my following, since the link was created between the object and the feeling of fear, you do not dare more to touch it, especially if this belief has strengthened year by year.

As a result, you no longer dare to learn for yourself because of forbidden things and do not know how certain objects work, and why other people can touch them.

The blockages come from there! There has always been, or at least often, someone above you, and that has prevented you from empowering, your parents or loved ones who have stopped you from doing it, discouraging you, saying that it is useless, or not taking seriously what you were doing because of your young age.

Also, you have become addicted to others because the slightest attempt to become a little more responsible will result in a lack of self-confidence, fear of reactions and mockery. How will everyone around you react? Will they find your way ridiculous? They will say that you are wasting your time? That feels the experience what I say there, huh?

Your entourage, being used to seeing you like this, with a low esteem, will probably not be ready to accept the changes that are taking place in your life if there are any, even if some congratulate you on your initiatives.

Others will criticize you, prepare for it, unless you remain disctretated, but with success, difficult to be, it remains a choice like any other with advantages and disadvantages, and there is and always will be a price to pay, then, what is your value?

How to gain confidence?

At what level are you compared to others? Whether friends, family, or hierarchical leaders, how do you feel in their presence?

In your environment, when you go to all those around you, you feel their energy unconsciously. It comes down to power or weakness, importance or non-importance. Each individual gives off energy. The intensity of each is felt. It's called "the aura".

Also, I invite you to do this little experiment, you will note all the feelings that you feel in contact with certain people, which they release of themselves. Is it intense? Less intense? Do they cause you joy or fear? Do not try with people you already know, but rather with strangers.

Do you have a high perception or a low perception of those around you? Clearly, do you feel someone strong or a shabby?

You too, you release your own energy and it feels outside.

When you are afraid of entering a dangerous neighborhood of a housing estate, what is going on inside you when you walk quietly very close to a group of young people? Do you feel anguish? These young people you do not know them, but something deep inside you created the feeling of oppression, as if something was going to happen, related to what you learned on TV talking about street assaults, in the clear you have associated this with the dangerousness of the environment.

Inwardly, you create harmful and destructive feelings, and everything that happens on the outside acts like a magnet, all because of your old beliefs.

Whether in parenting or school education, whether in your dating, there has always been someone above you, and unconsciously, you give reason to the fact that you feel small.

But by reconsidering things, an employer will

always be above you administratively, but you're too formalizing this. He may be superior, but he is no less a human being, you breathe the same air as he, he can die, hurt himself, experience emotions, outside social status and bank account, he is in every way identical to you.

By cons, you can change your angle of view on his person, how? By changing your perception, and in a way, try not to see an imposing person who gives you the feeling of being miniature, but little by little, making it miniature.

You'll imagine it in your head, and see it growing smaller, and relative to that, imagine yourself superior to it emotionally.

Unconsciously, and if you do this every night before going to bed, you will gain confidence, all the people you see who seem larger will become smaller, and you also say "I am higher than them! ".

But be careful, I'm not saying that you have to be superior, but feeling superior, that's the nuance, you're not going to interact with the outside world, but keep that feeling deep inside you!

Imagine a child, you are taller than him, you feel this greatness, what I ask you is to associate this feeling with a person you fear, see him as this child. And do not give more importance to his aura, what is needed is to grow yours.

By keeping this for you, you will observe what happens over several days, your perception will not be the same, the delicate relationships between your employer and yourself will diminish until you feel at the same level as him emotionally, he will be less on your back, and may even be inviting you to take coffee with him. (I know what I mean!).

Do not be trapped in your old beliefs that forced you to always perceive someone above you, imagine an emotional line. To a child, you will have a higher frequency, conversely, towards a business leader or a minister, you will have a lower frequency, which I try to make you understand, and that is why I repeat myself in order for you to understand what is wrong, it will not be possible, or perhaps difficult for you to conceive of success if you feel lower than a boss who inspires you with fear!

You are the hostage of a system of beliefs that limit you because, being very small, you always had someone above you! Are you still a kid? No ! So, straighten your shoulders, and be proud of yourself!

Suppose the following, if you want to become a millionaire, how do you perceive the rich honestly? Do they inspire you with fear? Power? Of the authority ? If you feel these emotions deep inside you, you will not reach this higher level. What's more, if you criticize them, it's the image of your future "you" that you criticize!

Become the leader and not the follower!

It is not too late ! You can take back your life in hand, there is no leader or follower, but everyone can become one or the other, if one decides to live a little more for oneself and not according to the dictate your surroundings. Your life belongs to you and you only have one, learn to use it well!

The leader takes on him, he never blames others, so he rectifies. This is defined by a person who assumes full responsibility for his actions, and enjoys no form of comfort zone, if something happens, he has the ability to cash without ever faltering. As for the follower, he is the exact opposite, he prefers to have someone who assumes his place, it can be a line manager, a colleague, a friend or a member of his family.

At first, eliminate the bad habit of saying that it is the faults of others, things are so made, we can not change the past, but focus on a better future, then, will come the degree of commitment to what you want to do, are you ready enough to go beyond? Are you ready to enhance your inner value?

Learn to become responsible! By becoming it, at the same time, you will become independent, and as I like to remind you, your life belongs to you alone, and it is your responsibility to build it without worrying about the opinion of others. !

One becomes responsible in learning to no longer be dependent on others, at least, mitigate the tendency to need someone for things that are accessible to all, is to have this ability to take on oneself.

Emotional perception

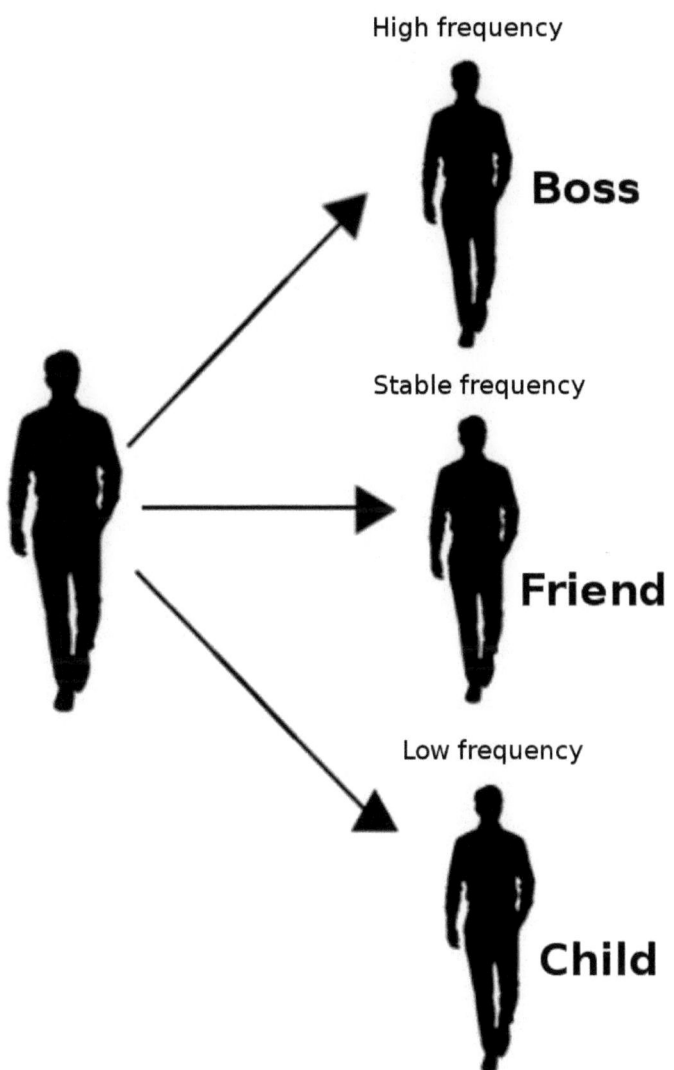

High frequency

Boss

Stable frequency

Friend

Low frequency

Child

Learn from one's mistakes

In life, we all make mistakes, and we can not be consistent in clearing customs when that happens, and reporting them to others, events, or the environment in general, it's not about staying above, and to question themselves.

One way to evolve and learn from your mistakes, to take on yourself by becoming responsible and to tell you that you are still alive because nothing is lost, you can always rectify.

They are part of life's experiences and they have strengthened you, and somewhere you are stronger than you think!

The whole thing is not to get stuck on it, but to move forward thanks to them. Well used, mistakes can be your best allies, because they give you that little extra than all the great leaders ... .experience.

Thomas Edison is a good example of this, he has been taken up many times in the subjects of personal development see where you may have already noticed!

His invention, which serves us in everyday life, that is to say, the light bulb, brings us light, was born from a succession of failures, but instead of giving up, he continued over and over, using the lessons of his mistakes until he got a result. It took him 10,000 attempts to get there.

It was the same for all that constitutes the modern world, especially in the aeronautics for example, the engineers did not focus because there were air crashes, on the contrary, they constantly sought to learn how to make planes safer.

The mistakes are to be taken as a lesson and not as a punishment, and they are not a flaw, but a way to evolve, remember this!

Social circles

Our world is home to more than seven billion people, all of us come from different backgrounds, whether professional or social, We all form this set that we call "Human Society".

These circles represent the different layers of human society and each circle includes different cultural, social or professional groups.

Somewhere in these circles, you and I are on different levels.

As for the level of the environment, it is about the average environment, the one where the majority of the individuals evolve, and to pass from one level to another, it is necessary to have two qualities, the curiosity and the will.

You rub shoulders with the same entourage, do the same things tirelessly every day, hang out in the same places, but do you ever think outside the box? See people who have succeeded in their life? It would be really instructive for you, and it would signify a significant evolution of your life, in other words, to see something else and expand the field of your knowledge (both cultural and human).

So, I invite you to do the following thing:

Pass the upper tier! What do I mean by that? This is one of the reasons why you do not evolve, because you unconsciously do the same things all the time, and it's time for you to realize it!

By doing something different, we are perfecting ourselves little by little, leading us to the desired goal, but for that, there are conditions, founding principles that work in your inner environment.

Whatever you do, and if you do not follow all that has just been mentioned in this book, you will relentlessly fall into the same pattern, and as I said on another chapter, it is again, and again , and again, why?

Unconsciously, you have created "your world"! The environment in which you evolve is a true copy of what you are inside. But it's not your fault, because you acted on the information you received from your childhood, and consolidating them growing up.

You are involuntarily your own creator.

My remarks may shock, but it is the sad reality, you are trained without your knowledge in a process that must unfortunately take its course, you can not erase the steps that allow you to move from one environment to another, you must let it finish.

Which is why you go from chess to failure in your projects, because you are still in the negative spiral, and whatever you do, even reading 100 books on the subject that I evoke, nothing will happen in your life ! The bills will always be paid, those to whom you owe money will not make you a gift as if by magic, my name is Yoann MERITZA and not David COPPER-FIELD.

I explain the procedure to follow, but that does not mean that nothing will happen, it is simply that it is not the right moment, you are charged negatively (I do not know which level you are exactly) but if you do exactly what I told you in this book, there will be changes that will happen, not overnight, but gradually following a guideline, a process to follow.

It will come naturally, and there is no point in being discouraged, because what you hope for is engaged in the positive spiral, but will come to an end at some point, because the positive cycle will end briefly, what to do, it's repeating the operation, maybe even 10,000 times as Mr Edison did, take slaps, but continue anyway, the positive circle will grow if you have deep inside you a lot of determination.

The first thing to do is to raise your self-esteem by telling yourself that you are superior to a boss, boss or other, not verbally, but deep inside you, give yourself value, you can do it! It is this ability to change one's perception, to be morally situated!

The second is to respect his entourage, to give them love, again, not necessarily verbally, but to learn to appreciate all those around you! Do not forget that your entourage is your reflection!

Stop criticizing, judging or complaining! What happens when you complain? You re-create the same circumstances each time, as when you say you're out of luck, the universe will answer you "yes! You're unlucky ! ". What you send to the universe will be returned to you in its material or immaterial equivalent, which prevents the universe from offering you what you desire is that in spite of you, you are still in a great vicious circle and as long as you do not do not mitigate by having positive thoughts constantly, it will always be the same pattern for you! that is, failures on failures.

That's why I tell you to solve your problems at the beginning of the book, for this reason, and also not to have to rethink it.

Look no further for trouble and see the future with a fresh eye, do not give up your plans, continue, over and over, start again and again, always keeping in mind that this will happen, let the magic take place and when you are fairly positively charged, changes will occur until your projects are completed.

Of course, according to the law of polarity, there will always be a positive side, and a negative one, and there will be problems, but they will be of less importance. Just jolts that will subside very quickly.

CHAPTER 7:
DETACHMENT

"The mystery and wealth of the world of everyday life are second to none. And the conditions for accessing the wonders of this world are detachment, but also love and self-sacrifice. "
(Carlos Castaneda)

Here is a little inspiring story:

Paul invites his friends to go ballooning.

Everyone comes aboard, delighted to take a ride in the sky.

When taking off, Paul warms the air in the balloon so he can take flight.

Only here, the balloon remains nailed to the ground.

So, Paul asks his friends to let go of the ballast, but it still does not take off!

Intrigued, he asks his friends to free their bags to lighten the load. But nothing happens!

Paul does not understand! Why does not the balloon take off?

To lighten the gondola even further, he asks some of his passengers to get off, but nothing is happening.

The rest of his friends start to leave the gondola until he finds himself alone in it.

Then Paul tries one last time to take off the ball, full throttle this time, until there is more fuel.

The balloon begins to deflate on Paul to cover it!

In vain trying to get out of the basket, Paul stumbles on a rope, the one holding the balloon on the ground.

The moral of this story is that to evolve very high, even by releasing some weights and put-

ting full throttle, if we do not detach ourselves from our beliefs (the rope), we risk losing friends, and giving the maximum in these circumstances, we risk emptying his reserves.

Here is how the law of attraction works, as long as you are attached to your beliefs, you will not take off and risk losing everything!

The brain is programmed to meet certain habits of everyday life, do not you realize that you repeat the same things tirelessly?

What you are experiencing is what you think, because external events bring you to some form of belief, and the latter makes you see the outside world in a certain way.

In fact, everything turns in a loop, as locked in the same field of values without seeing anything or glimpses of other.

Your mind is in its very down-to-earth form, that is, to take into account what you have learned as true. What the universe sends you back is something you had previously accepted.

The subconscious has a security system in the form of blockages from your childhood.

Which means that for those who succeed and who see the world in a certain way, it seems consistent for them, but not for you, it seems absurd, unbelievable, and yet, between someone who succeeds and someone who one that fails, one thing remains the same, the world in which everyone lives, only the way to perceive things change.

You will see everything a successful person does, she never complains, brings back every event, and does not see the dark future. He is full of energy and as soon as he has a blow of weakness and doubts, it has this ability to get back in the saddle anyway.

Those who succeed have no limit other than that which they impose themselves, all because their frequency is certainly limited, but very high.

Ruminate the past and anticipate the future

Our human condition compels us to interpret events external to our thoughts.

One thing is certain, as an author, and I know it very well, for I guess, for the most part, a form of weariness in reading this book. On the one hand, you seem captivated to know what's coming next, but on the other hand, there's a tiny, barely perceptible voice that whispers "what's the point?" It will never work! ".

At first, when I wrote my very first book, I wondered why I was doing all this? I told myself that it was still one of my whims, well, in short, something inside me told me to give up, that it was useless!

Currently, I'm in my third book, I would not have even thought two or three years ago that I would be known in more than twenty countries with my books, that they would be translated into English and Spanish, and yet that's the case! I still happen to surprise me!

What are these little fragments of thoughts in your head? Do you have things in your life that catch you?

Do you have a negative person next to you who reminds you that you have to pay the gas bill or that she says "stop wasting your time with this book! Or "your mother has called you! "?

Do you think back to yesterday or a few hours ago?

Do you have snatches of memories that come to the surface?

Or do you think back to those around you who perceive you as a loser?

In your past, you had events powerful enough to impact your psyche. They made fun of you and pushed you into your entrenchments that caused that feeling of uneasiness, and as I said before, it must be an engine and not a brake! Learn how to reap the benefits.

There are two streams of thoughts in your mind, there is the hope of a better life by reading, you think you will find the solution to all your problems (what I'm trying to do bring it if you believe it!).

And on the other hand, you fear that it brings you nothing more, having read other authors in the same field as me, but the results have remained minimal, see zero.

All authors, regardless of the field, come from your outside world. Of course, as authors, we help you find solutions, of course everything that is proposed works, that said, we are not magicians, but there is great magic in you, and we give you the tracks to reach this magical source.

You say to yourself, "No, that's not it! And I would answer you: "Yes, that's exactly it! "

You are connected to a tiny, almost imperceptible form of thought that I would call "latent fear." It's something hidden in you, and you unconsciously do not suspect it's presence.

It even happens to travelers who fly quite often. They do not think about air crashes, at least they know it's potentially possible. I tell you, it is imperceptible and manifests itself in the form of an emotion.

It also happens to professionals, such as business leaders making a very good turnover, but having somewhere to remember a bitter failure last month.

It's like repainting in green a red wall, you think green, but subconsciously, you are thinking of red, the last color serving only to camouflage the first.

To no longer think about it, you must scratch the wall, remove all the red, and repaint in green, which will be the dominant layer in your mind, this is what is called "having an absolute faith".

What is happening, whether you like it or not, you are attached to your past, and that represents mostly the stages of your life, by the principle of positive or negative consolidation, a sequence of events that confirm certain beliefs and confirm others.

The present moment, self-esteem, detachment and positive focus are the pillars that will make you a winner.

At the same time, you are sure of yourself, and you have the germ of that fear inside you! That's why I gave you some instructions at the beginning of this book.

One of the fears is to see your projects sabotaged by others. Am I right?

What are you willing to do to change? Are you ready to start again the next day? Two days later ? What form of commitment do you have to this?

You want everything that comes from the second world, while remaining in the first, prisoner of a reality that you do not want.

Do not live in two different spheres, you will not attract anything if you do not give up ballast, the balloon will not take off the ground, get out of your comfort zone means out of his routine, his habits, become more responsible and not dependent on others.

It is impossible, even, very confused to think of two things at once, between wanting 1 million € and waiting for his salary, you understand that there is a form of contradiction? The universe does not know what you really want, it's like going to a restaurant, and the waiter is waiting for you to make your choice, and too hesitating, you end up with soup.

Detachment in this is very important! Let go of what you do not want anymore! Do you want to continue to wait for your salary at the beginning of the month? Or do you want to make more money? What amount? Be precise !

You are like the mass of people waiting for their pay, always in need of money, always thinking about their salary. You expect 1 million € and at the same time, you expect 1500 € (assuming it is your monthly salary), and that's where I tell you it's pretty confusing.

Do you often look at your bank account to check if your salary has arrived? Do not do it anymore, because it blocks you in the same pattern, the one you do not want anymore! The one that prevents you from moving forward! If all goes well on your bank account, you do not need to look at it, and to take the example of the balloon, there is no point in letting go of the ballast if you do not detach the rope, and it is also a problem for you, you are attached to this same scheme.

Normally, by paying your debts and paying attention to your expenses, you do not have to constantly look at your bank account, this too, is a loser attitude, always worried about how much remains, and this is in disagree with your deepest desire.

We can not put ourselves in phase, that is to say, have the feeling of having already his deepest desire, to say that we are prosperous while the external events prove you the opposite (call of the bank or bailiff's mail, for example).

Avoid mined land, such as compulsive shopping on fraudulent sites, avoid spending on unknown sites and only go to trusted sites, asking yourself this question "why do you want to make this purchase?"

Avoid taking what you do not really need at the supermarket.

Adopt a healthy lifestyle, but I'm not asking you to deprive yourself of everything, a small gap, it can happen, but it should not be excessive.

By living in two spheres, the real world and the world in which you want to live, as I said before, your thoughts must remain authentic, and that all the time, even after successful, do not fall back into the trap of the life you had before!

Look around you!

Apart from the debts you will pay (as suggested above), with a little hindsight, what is wrong with your life? Nothing ! Absolutely nothing !

ALL
GO
WELL !

The only limits are those that we impose!

If for example, you are a player, each week, you make a small lotto grid "for fun" say you!

But unconsciously lies the hope of winning the jackpot (stop lying to yourself!)

So I can tell you right now that you will never win, or at least, small amounts consistent with your PARADIGM..

You are programmed to lose! Sad reality, but that's exactly it!

How beautiful it is to dream of the lottery jackpot, to offer the expected life, far from "worries" and "debts" (I voluntarily support these words because just to evoke it, you think about it!).

Does that mean that everything is hardly lost? No !

To win the jackpot (and not hope), you must have "THE FAITH"

It's a difficult concept to master!

To help you understand the magnitude of the problem, I invite you to put your salary on all games of chance.

Do you want to understand how scared you will be? You will not dare to take the plunge, because a whole system of thoughts starts in connection with your programming, your "PARADIGM".

This is exactly what happens on a smaller scale, the fear of losing your bet "is well and truly there! "With the possibility of earning small sums while having the desire to earn millions, you understand a little better what is happening? It's pretty confusing inside you, and your ideas are not very clear.

Your past experiences have taken precedence in your life, you have scratched game tickets or ticked numbers, even following the horoscope, nothing has changed, and it has become a recurring habit in your subconscious. If this has always been so, why would this change?

Without asking too many questions, why and how will this happen (as this will happen if you have "confidence").

have "faith" !

What is faith ? It is to have absolute confidence (an "Unlimited Confidence" as the title of the book of Franck Nicolas), in what one does, without worrying about the consequences.

To have faith is not only "I believe in this or that"

To have faith is to make the detachment from the earth down, this programming of the paradigm!

It's the air you breathe, for example, without asking yourself why you do it, you have faith in it.

You must learn first and foremost to cultivate the positive in you and around you, and to be enthusiastic about each event in order to charge you with positive energy.

Then, pretend that everything we desire was already within our reach both in the imagination and in the feeling.

The money you hope exists in a bank account in your mind, live with this idea in mind, it will become real if you do not hope! Let go and keep this in a corner of your head, live with that feeling that everything you expect, you already have it!

Think of a beautiful house as if you already had it, cultivate the feeling of accomplishment and pride, it is yours! Know that somewhere, she is real!

But in no case should you give a feeling of impatience and hope, for there will be a contradiction between wanting something and having it already.

Cultivate ONLY the feeling of "having already"!

From this moment your spirit will be in harmony with your desire, you will vibrate on the right frequency, with the cinae condition do not tell you that you are doing this (all that I explained to you) in order to obtain!

Just think about it by cultivating the intimate conviction that you already have it! Just this! Practice this for several days to convince your paradigm! A time needed would be about a month to integrate this new program!

Inhale and exhale, then learn to look and hear the world differently, do not be destabilized by what can happen in the outside world! Detach from this!

Improve your present relationships by not thinking about the future, take full advantage of the present moment, focus only on this by having healthy thoughts of kindness.

All will be well if you follow scrupulously what I already mentioned.

Do not pay attention to criticism

The people you meet in your life are used to your way of being and they can tell themselves that it is not possible otherwise.

When our environment changes, it disturbs our environment, not knowing how to respond to these changes, and eventually adapt to our way of being, giving a destructive response to what we are, pushing us into difficult entrenchments overcome. They are essentially jealous people, unable to take care of themselves, and they feel miserable in the face of someone they consider weak.

Those who criticize are those who have not even tried, and do not admit that you can go beyond them, while they stay in their comfort zone, always living in envy and criticism.

The evolution of your life will be perceived as a joke by malicious people, how someone so daring dares you want to exceed us?

A personal story that allowed me to turn my weaknesses into strengths, which gave me inspiration, critics are a very good tool:

When I even took the initiative to write books on the subject of personal development, I knew that I would be subject to the most harsh criticism, but on the other hand, if I did not operate change, nothing would evolve in my life. I took risks, but if we do not do it, who will do it for us?

Criticism comes mainly from your social circle. To do this, be careful not to display your project (s) in the open, and start orienting yourself towards socially successful people, such as managers and traders, you will see that you will be encouraged, however, if you reveal your intentions directly to those around you, from a modest background (and here I'm not talking about the family that will support you if she learned it), they will find this ridiculous and laugh at you even before 'reach the first ounce of success

Clearly, build your future without worrying about others, and surround yourself with good people

Let success come to you, and it will come if you believe it enough.

If success is there, those who criticize you will jealous you, but also, in time, this jealousy will be part of the past if you know how to put the forms, and will become a pride to know you, because everyone will follow your model.

What was a fear will turn into enthusiasm, and on the other hand, having been entitled to criticism (as all successful ones know), I ended up accepting them.

And I will go further by saying that it is precisely the critics who have allowed me to make myself known, which is quite paradoxical.

The conclusion to all this is that one must trust one's instinct, and receive the good or bad opinions of others, because both are important.

Whether you are known for good or bad, you are known anyway, and like me, you will be known in more than twenty countries in the world (even beyond).

Criticism is useful, it allows some skeptics, sharpened with curiosity, to make their own opinion, so to speak "sell".

All opinions are selling, do not forget it!

That's why in my first two books, I told you to turn your weaknesses into strengths, and that, when you think about it, it's useful to write down everything you remember, in order to analyze what kind of behavior you had at that moment, then reinterpret that event you remember.

Let me ask you a few questions:

Those people who hurt you in the past, have you seen them recently?

If so, is their life better than yours?

Why did they act in one way with you, and not on another? By need of belonging? To repress an evil being on you?

This greatly deepens what you are, your past with certain individuals who have been harmful to you, due to beliefs instilled by your parents or relatives, or simply events that have had a cognitive impact associated with a feeling, that have given you information about how to behave in good or bad, and this has been etched in your mind and amplified by events of the same nature.

The fear of others has been destructive to you, and has had a direct impact on both your romantic and professional relationships.

Yomer's theory

Some time ago, I wrote a book called "How to reprogram your subconscious? Or I evoked the theory of Ping-pong ball, or otherwise called in personal development "The Yomer Theory".

To summarize without much talk about it, imagine a glass of water that represents your universe, water symbolizes a poor environment, one in which most people evolve, and looks like a rich environment that many would like to reach.

The ping pong ball represents your inner world, it gives you a perception of the universe according to what you have learned, experienced or felt.

This ping pong ball has several inner layers, representing every aspect of your life.

If all the aspects are filled with water, which represents poverty, the ball will remain at the bottom of the glass, in a water environment, and conversely if they are filled with air (rich environment or objective to reach).

The kernel represents the paradigm, it is all that you have recorded as information from the first days of your existence. Your value judgments and related feelings are part of it. This is the first neuro-associability (or matrix), or all the new information will be added, they will grow like the roots of a tree in your brain.

Another author in the field of personal development, James Hilman, has written a book called "The Secret Code of Your Destiny" where he explains the principles of "the Aken" (the "kernel"), the source that provoked a series of events taking us where we are.

What happens in the outside world affects your state of mind, keep a form of living space for you!

Learn to be like the ping pong ball, with a waterproof shell, the water can not infiltrate it, you have the mind of a winner, which makes you a loser, it's your permeability, letting in the negative feelings and events from the outside. It is impossible to change your condition if you think of two things at the same time.

It's as if life is putting us to the test when we pay too much attention to the outside world. For you, it is essential to refocus and be water-proof, you can not hide the problem, but do not take it as such, look for solutions, and see the future with progress and challenges.

Theory of the Ping-pong ball

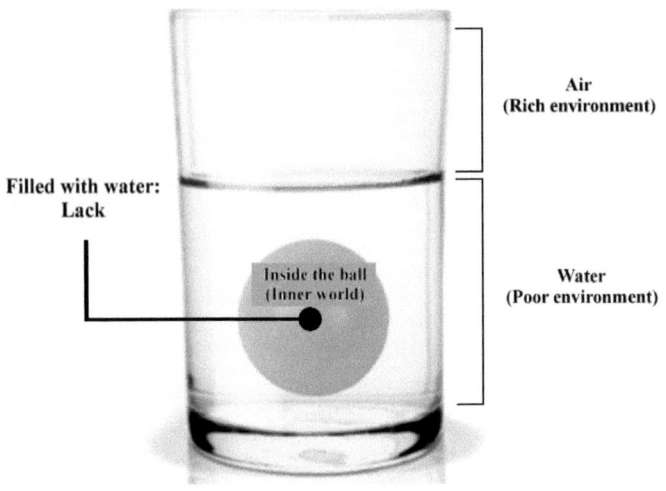

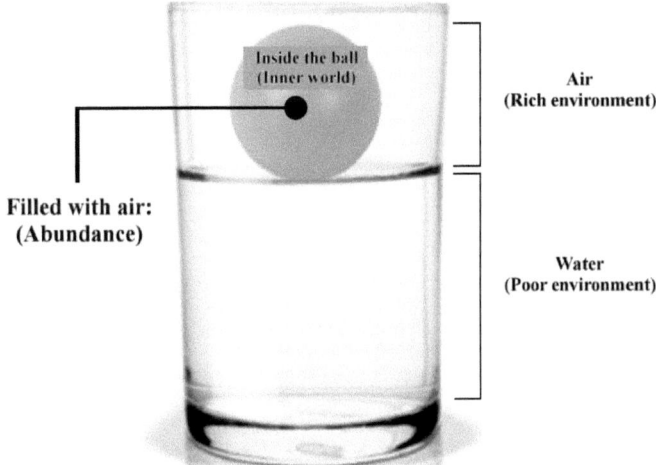

The junction of the two worlds

Within our being are two environments, one is in the perception of the outside world according to the interpretation that you make of it according to your old schema, presenting limiting beliefs related to the paradigm, and there is the other part of your imagination is what allows the process of creation, to give shape with your hands to reveal our artistic side.

Right now, you're in between, on the one hand, you have all the down-to-earth aspects of what you perceive with your consciousness, it's your reality, it's the world you live in, or the least, the interpretation you have of it.

And then there is your imagination that allows you to create a universe sweetened with little elves in a wonderful country. The imaginary allows us to become who we want, a prosperous person, loved by all, who cares nothing.

We are, in large part, responsible for our reality, both at the level of the people we meet and the unfortunate circumstances of our lives.

Remember at the beginning of the book, I asked you to solve your problems in order to facilitate the attractive power that is in you, because according to your way of thinking, all that happens is the product of your mind, which has created a magnetism between what you do not want and yourself.

In all circumstances and at all times, we send signals to the universe, thus creating the osmosis of converging frequencies (I do not know if I am very clear!).

In order to create the optimal conditions for the law of attraction to work, it is to first settle your current problems, it is your contribution, and it will allow to have the mind clear to change the course of your thoughts, because that's what it's about.

First of all, you will imagine the world that would be ideal for you, if you want a sports car, a very big house, money, and everything you want! Do not forget to specify which types of relationships you want, and how you perceive your surroundings in this ideal.

Keep this little world in a corner of your head, it will serve for what will follow.

Then, while standing, you will draw a large circle with your hands, starting from the top to the bottom. There, you drew the outlines of your world in the reality of the outside world.

In this circle, with your hand (left or right), you will act as if you were taking an element of your ideal (make the gesture with your hand as if you were taking it in your head), to throw it into "your world, "then you will think of a new reality, with this incorporated ideal. Then you will convince yourself that this is really part of the outside world.

Inhale and exhale convincing yourself of this new reality.

The outside world is you who created it, your new "world", you also create it following the same process.

The universe is infinite, there is no limit in the outside world, since you are "the creator" of it. It is imperative to convince oneself of this.

Do the same with the other elements of your ideal, throw them in "your world", then you will focus on it, try to convince yourself that it is part of your outer world.

Then, you will advance close to this circle, breathe the air on the other side, feel the emotions it emanates, soak up your ideal, "your world" planted in the middle of the reality of the outside world, then you will act as if you are entering a door, you are at the doorway of these, breathe and feel again, it is you who create all this, and with your mind. You return to your ideal that becomes your reality, all around you, without you seeing it is changing.

What I just described must now be part of you, shake your head or pass under the water, this is your reality, I know that for the moment, it looks exactly to the old schema of your life, but if you continue to perceive it so, to the extent that you keep it deep inside you, do not tell anyone for now, let things change little by little, keep the same new beliefs, and I assure you that they will come true, it takes a period of between 30 and 90 days depending on the individuals to see the metamorphoses of the outside world.

This has been your creation since birth, it is your creation, and it will be it again and again, only the circumstances that have changed, an inversion of the polarities of your existence.

Also, to stay in this realism of your ideal, have a perception in 3 dimensions, between what you think of others and what others think of you, and what you think of yourself, of how you feel perceived . Feel like someone different and all around you will be, if you focus on that for a little while, you will be convinced in the long run without struggling to try to convince you.

As I said, there is a real magic in you, and the frequency that you will emit will be in osmosis with that of your desires in the universe.

191

If you understand correctly, you will bring your imagination back into your reality, and feel this as true, and it will materialize if you follow exactly what I told you.

What you think is an integral part of your reality

Old reality

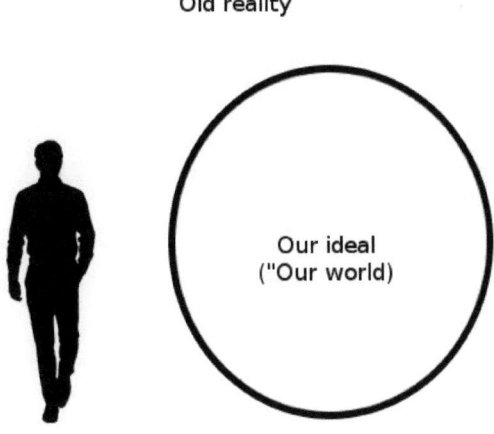

Our ideal
("Our world)

Integration in our
new reality

**Real world
(conscious)**

**Imaginary
(unconscious)**

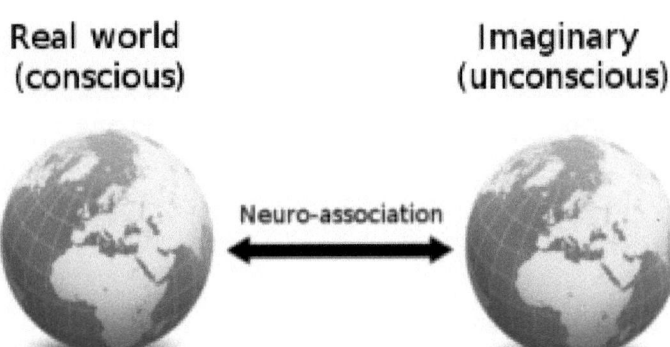

Neuro-association

Convergence of the two worlds

Gestation of the new reality
(duration between 30 and 90 days)

PART II:
PUT INTO PRACTICE

CHAPTER 8: TIPS FOR THE LAW OF ATTRACTION TO WORK

"Whatever happens, always keep your mind above the line! "
(Yoann MERITZA)

We will tackle a very important phase devoted to the law of attraction. But before you talk about it, take the strong commitment in you to stick to it.

Warning ! For what follows, I will ask you the greatest attention. What I am going to tell you will bring you to whatever you want if you stay focused.

Throughout this book, I have transmitted all my knowledge in the field of the law of attraction, this part offers you all the methods to cause events that will change your life. I would like the person you will become more prepared for a better future and be surprised by all progress you can make. The next year will not be comparable anymore, because you will have reached a level above. At the bottom of you lies a hidden treasure, and with every change in your life, you dig a little deeper to discover your abilities, because for me, you are capable of it! You will be able to prove it to yourself, by changing habits, you will become another person, an improved being able to prove himself that he can always reach a notch above (above the line).

The method that I propose to you is to pass several levels of our existence before reaching the fullness, this one can take several forms, I will dissect with you one by one, all the levels approach you progressively of your objectives.

It's about changing one habit at a time, anchoring it well before moving on to the next one. When it is well into your daily life, you will have passed the next level.

How to proceed ? I will give you a list of tasks to be done, each of which should last at least a month, then, with this new habit, combine another.

1) Fix your problems so you do not have to think about them again, and do not spend extra money:

I know that in a month everything will not be solved, but that you are in phase to do it! During this period, you will look for all possible solutions to repay all your debts. Until this is fixed, you will constantly rethink it.

No longer looking for problems, they come mainly from lack, and in attractiveness, this is synonymous with failure.

It's better to have than to want, make a list of everything you have, health, a job, a roof over your head ...

Stop living constantly in the pattern of need! You have things at home that you would like to replace, because some of them do not please you anymore, or it becomes obsolete.

What happens when you want to change a piece of furniture or the TV, even by visualizing these objects, your paradigm catches you and whispers "yes, but with what money are you going to pay for this? Or how do you intend to get there? It is not obvious to want everything with a sword of Damocles in mind, in these conditions, it is unlikely to produce real change with in mind the possibility of the visit of a usher or a recommended form the bank. Understand that if you think of prosperity at the same time as you think of your debts, there is a form of incompatibility between these two forms of thinking.

You have in you a little mental lock that puts you back on the ground, in this reality shaped by the paradigm.

It's an unresolved thing in your mind, and life events make you think back, whether it's family issues, at your level, your environment or others

Even if you adopt the attitude of seeing only the positive, it is as if you trusted the road, right in front of you, while having the fear of a puncture or engine failure.

2) Read two books a month

You will get used to read books, even if only a few pages a day (twenty, it's already not bad), spend a moment of your day, at least an hour to this, it is possible on 24 hours, I have always said and I will always say, culture will serve you all the time, and for me, there is a real magic in the reading, because it radically changes your state of mind, giving you the feeling superior, eliminating doubts about philosophical topics for example!

Culture brings people together, and you will meet people who will be the actors of your future life (themselves cultivated), leading you into a new social schema. And concretely, even if you have long-time friends, what do you really bring? Have they evolved, are they rich? Or do they stagnate in their difficulties? It can be believed what I claim, but it is not the people you meet in your daily life that will change your social condition, because you are part of the same pattern, While if you start reading and you go to the libraries, you will meet more interesting people, and that will change your social links.

Nothing requires you to read only books on personal development, you can vary by reading other topics, such as philosophy, Kant, Nietzsche, Plato, Confucius, or you can improve in English, French, Math , or in history. The whole thing is not trying to understand at all costs what is in these books, but to operate a process of repetition by reading several books of the same theme, you will see, there will be an impression of already seen, because unconsciously, you will have retained a part, and this phase of repetition fills the rest.

It's like seeing a statue in a museum, seeing it from the front is good, but just change the angle of view, looking at the sides, behind, in short, on all of its seams to see the integral work with precision in your mind.

Your knowledge will grow and your confidence will also improve your beliefs. The more you get into the habit of reading daily, the more you will be hungry for knowledge.

Force yourself to do it! Although I know that for some of you, it is boring to read, seeing the number of pages or the content of them.

And yet, you read mine, what is this different? The subject I use is passionate, but do not confine yourself to this one, the world of culture is very vast, so get off the beaten path!

By reading small end by little end (20 to 30 pages per day), as you go, you will not even think about the number of pages so you will be absorbed, and also, you will not even think about your problems, it will become a daily habit, and I would say better than that, it will become a pleasure, it will bring you a lot, especially as you charge your energies positively (provided you do not read novels called "black").

Your senses will be awake and you will feel every word in you.

If I can recommend something, insist strongly during the first month, it will allow time for your mind to get used to this change of pace on a daily basis, very little in sync with this habit.

In addition to this, you also have TV channels that offers scientific and cultural programs, even if they are not interesting, try to watch at least one show, just to arouse your curiosity, on the construction of dams by beavers, does anyone know how their buildings are actually made?

I propose you to do the following test:

Write a sentence on a piece of paper!

Write down what you want, which comes to your mind.

Fold it in 4, and put this piece of paper in a secret place, and above all, play the game!

Do not read it for a period of one year.

Start reading books quietly during this time

and then take out your piece of paper on which you have written the phrase of your choice!

Do you find what you noted is absurd? It's normal ! You have evolved!

One of the ways to realize how far you've come, you can be proud of yourself, your spirit has grown!

But I'm not saying to stop at this after one year, you can continue throughout your life, in one year, you will have read 24 books, and much more after, I hope for you.

3) No longer see his dark future

We must cultivate living in the present moment and focus on the positive. As I said earlier in this book, remember that you are the creator of your destiny, and what you think determines what you are! The universe always responds to the actuality of your thoughts, and your thoughts are consolidated by what the universe sends back to you, that is to say, what you sent to it. Said like that, I understand that it looks complicated, but let me develop!

What happens is a form of osmosis between your way of thinking and the universe, everything is in constant balance from birth to now, the way you perceive things is exactly as you have suggested it voluntarily or not, and also, you will always be plagued by this vicious circle if you do not change your perception of things! It will be again, again, and again!

For example, if you've never had a chance in life, that's what you're saying deep inside you, it's a belief that has been around for a very long time in your mind, and you're saying, "why it would be otherwise? ".

This deep conviction sends a signal back to the universe and responds to you effectively and in balance with that type of thought.

Try to think otherwise by telling yourself that you are lucky, feel what you think and try to convince yourself to weaken this vicious circle that will remain very present for a little while! External circumstances are what they are, you will not be able to change them in a snap, everything is part of a longer or shorter process, but you can perceive yourself differently, as someone who attracts luck.

Have the constant idea that everything is going well! Repeat it in you mentally and verbally while whispering "everything is going well! In the moment, focus only on that. Especially if you have followed my recommendations and you have settled your debts (or about to be solved), and you treat your friends. What are the reasons that would push you to rethink? Nothing ! Because everything is fine and everything should be fine.

Also, do not over-watch media like BFMTV with what is happening in Paris today with yellow vests or disaster-related newspapers, nothing prevents you from keeping yourself informed, but not over the long term, it influences your Moral and see everything in black if you feel involved, it is better to look at this with a lot of hindsight and tell yourself that things will improve for you.

Do not worry about the next day and see them differently, by repeating the magic phrase, every day in your head at least ten times a day when you wake up "Today is a good day, the best of all and tomorrow, it will be better and better ! And then, in the evening, before going to bed, feel gratitude for this day, whatever the outcome. How? In thanking the universe of lessons you have learned, because there are no negative things at all, these are just clues that the universe gives you in order to rectify certain situations. These are mainly jolts of your old pattern that will have to diminish over time, you have the opportunity to rectify. Do not fall into the trap of this old scheme (the one you do not want anymore). Trust the universe, it is there to help you, even if the circumstances show the opposite.

4) Stop complaining

Enjoy everything you have, be happy and grateful for what life has to offer.

Learn to be grateful to life itself, because in spite of everything that happens, we often forget the essential, the power of interaction with the outside world, something we can not do once we die.

As long as there is life, there is hope, and those who complain about their misfortunes should take a closer look at the eminent Dr. Hawking, who was a very great scientist, and that despite his handicap.

The body is the physical manifestation of the mind and when you understand this, all possibilities are open to you!

Be already grateful for what you already have, do not miss anything, learn to live well in the present moment, with serenity, in order to get more from the universe! The present moment is "THE" essential key that you will open the doors to success.

If you do not like what you have, how can you love what you will have?

Also, words and thoughts have power over the circumstances of your existence, which means that every time you complain, you send the universe a signal associated with an emotion.

For example, to think that one has no luck risks precisely creating the conditions for which you do not have one!

It's the same for those who think that men are like this, or women are like that, if they have a priori on some people, they will not be surprised to find themselves alone.

The same goes for those who complain about the rich, while they have the deep desire to become one, do not forget, the universe is a gigantic mirror.

So, stop complaining! Love the people around you! Whether rich or poor, do not forget that these are the reflections of yourself!

5) Wish the best for your surroundings

As curious as it may seem, even if the relationship is tense with those around you, I would ask you not to judge them and wish them the best (even if they already have it, and that they are at a better level than you).

The more you wish to see others rise, the more you will rise in your turn, and what is more, if you want things to improve for them, it also means that they will not ask you anything. They will be happy with what they have and will not solicit you for help or others. Maybe they will help you climb, but I do not guarantee anything on it!

Ask your boss for a promotion to your boss that his business is working, and if it turns out well for them, it's the same for you, because a business that goes wrong is synonymous with dismissal somewhere. Do not want the boat to sink while you're on board! Use your heart and be authentic with what you want!

In the universe, it's better to be the second roped than the first, there are people able to pull you up, rather than to climb alone on a mountain of difficulties.

To summarize, what you will do for others, you will do for yourself.

In everyday life, we meet all kinds of people, some help us to progress, such as school teachers, and others teach us (voluntarily or not) to regress, either by thinking well or by lack confidence (this second case generally applies to narcissists).

For those who make us regress, it happens in the form of criticism, always to jealous the success of others or to belittle the weakest of mind, you are then in the grip of so-called "toxic" beings, who are very gifted to undermine our morale as soon as we pay attention to their derogatory remarks. As a result, by entering into their game, they have power over us and prevent us from evolving, they are people who have a low self-esteem, and always have the need to seek in others a form of power of submission.

Also, it is important, if you start a work of transformation of your mind, to avoid the contact of this type of individuals and to ignore them.

Even if the remarks can reach you, you say that it is the aim sought by the authors of these, learn to ignore them and to trust you!

If you think you can do more than others can claim, then you really are.

6) Do not judge, criticize or insult

"Man is an animal for man! As a famous quote would say.

You will change the relationships you have with your outside world. I know that in the beginning it will not be easy, but you have to fight with your old inner demons. Dale Carnegie advocates it in her book "How to make friends ?".

As I have already mentioned, it is you who are building your outer world from your inner world, this is the phenomenon of synchronicity, and you still do it now, what you live everyday is still in phase with the universe.

When you are too focused on yourself, your environment sends you the same signal. That is to say, you meet people who are too focused on themselves and you will only attract that, in short, we will not be interested in you, as shocking as it can be said.

Be very careful on this point, you risk producing concordances with your old schema, that is to say that now that I have told you that, you will say "Owl! It's fastoche! ". In fact, if there is one point that the universe likes and above all, it's authenticity.

"Do not play the game to play the game! Because behind the desire to be interested in others, if you do it to improve your little person, it will not work! Why ? You are still in a ego schema, do not do it because I tell you, but only if you know how to show "SINCERITE".

Put yourself in the shoes of those around you! Would you like to be judged, criticized or insulted? Unconsciously, even if some people say no, you do it! (I assure you, yes!)

If you put your heart on it; as you learn to understand people, you will discover why they are like that!

I'm not asking you to give in to their requests to help them in case of a hard blow, just to understand and appreciate them despite their flaws.

the universe is composed of two worlds, one is internal to each living being, and the other external, these two worlds function according to the same resonance.

First, time, you have the power to control the past, the present and the future. By reconsidering all the feelings related to childhood? The learning you had from life. Your own experiences and the meaning you gave them.

Then, in space, because you are part of a whole, the inner and outer world communicate with each other on the same frequencies, those you send are identical to those you receive!

If you underestimate yourself, or if you underestimate another person, it will come back to you sooner or later, or it is still happening in your day-to-day life, so be careful what you send in the book. Universe!

Take the test! How many times have you criticized or insulted those around you? It can be words or thoughts (pay attention to both!). Take on the fait accompli by trapping yourself!

Put a recorder near you, in your pocket or on a table and let the recorder run for a while, then go back to your business or chat with a friend.

You will also see that even your friends will push you most often to criticism, do not enter the game!

Rewind and listen to yourself talking with your friend or friends about a co-worker, for example.

"- I saw" so-and-so *"today, he had an old coat on him and looked like a poor fellow!*

- It is true ! What a poor guy! "

Just this sentence can bring you the same circumstances as the individual you are talking about, even if you think about it, re-educate yourself and learn to respect people, even if the circumstances do not lend themselves to it.

I'm not saying that the example reflects exactly what is being said around you, but at some point in our daily lives we can not prevent ourselves from judging negatively, directly or indirectly, it is in our nature.

Be constructive with healthier thoughts and self-analysis! Is not everything that happens to you in your life the result of a behavior that you had before, a few weeks ago, or in the more distant past, and whose fruits you still reap?

The problem lies only in you, in what you

learn and in what you learn by judging and being judged.

Avoid the toxic people by wishing them that their situation changes. What you say is positive to others will have an impact on you, and if you believe it enough, even if the relationship with the toxic people does not change, there will be a form of magic in you, this thing that will allow you to to evolve, because you will have wished the best to the others, and conversely, those who criticized you will have only what they will send you. In any case, you will not have to wish them any misfortune, it may fall on you.

Interested in others and you will become interesting in the eyes of the world.

Take a step back to focus only on yourself, and also, you must be airtight, live in your inner world, the world is so and you can not change it. However, you can change to shoot everything around you to your advantage.

In what position do you want to be in relation to him? An actor or a spectator? A leader or a follower?

7) *Have another perception of oneself*

You are both an actor and a spectator of your existence!

If the world around us perceives us in a certain way, it is only the consequence of what you have sent to others, this return of image has affected you, creating in you your own demons.

Only you have created this situation unconsciously, and even if you were too young to remember it, it's not just words or thoughts, but also a priori, the way you feel the individuals who create your world.

However, there is the possibility of reversing the trend, first of all, we must learn to love ourselves, accept ourselves as we are, and we can improve.

Also, judging everything around you acts like

a foil, there is a lot of magic just as there can be a lot of witchcraft in your feelings.

You only know one world, the one you have created, by attracting people and circumstances directly to your inner world.

See the others as they would like to see you, and try to have their eyes. The world that surrounds you is a reflection of who you are. Remember that the universe is a gigantic mirror and you are the mirror of the universe.

In connection with what I mentioned earlier, we will play a game, but this time, nothing to write, everything happens in your subconscious.

At first, try to imagine the individual who would be in front of you, this can be an acquaintance, a member of the family or others, How do you perceive yourself? For good or for bad ? What is he wearing ? How does he talk to you? Describe the person in you in your subconscious!

For the exercise to work, it will be necessary to think of two types of individuals, one above and one below you socially.

You will try to imagine yourself in front of yourself, act as if you are looking in a mirror, if we assume that each individual and events are a reflection of ourselves

Just slip into the skin of a person who is in front of you.

Try to detail yourself from head to toe, what clothes do you wear? How do you seem to be? Introverted or extroverted? How do you express yourself?

For the one below you, describe her in detail, her gestures, her way of expressing herself, of moving, what she wears as clothes (her style), then, try to put yourself in her place, and of describe yourself according to your own criteria

Observe how you react, move and express yourself, and you will see your own flaws.

Do the same with the person who is above you socially, take his place and observe! Why does your boss behave in a certain way with you?

You will come to understand your own problems. If you have this ability to see in others what is wrong with you.

What would be the points to improve according to you in what you are? Your clothes ? Your behavior? The way to express yourself?

With the outside look, try to criticize yourself, and find through the eyes of others what should be improved!

Practice in front of a mirror, with the camera of your smartphone or your tape recorder

Try to improve your person and direct him towards your ideal, according to how others would like to perceive you, by taking stock of your faults and by trying to correct them, you will learn to love you more and more, your relations are not will only be better and you will be appreciated for these small changes (even minor ones), and so what you have become.

A phase of your beliefs about yourself will change, learning to love you.

Observe the positive aspects of these people by telling them that it is always possible for them to improve or to appreciate you looking for the qualities in others, and in return, these same people will find you.

experience the positive in negative people, you will discover a treasure.

8) Change your inner world

All of what you do or what you did, defines what you are!

Learn to change yourself before trying to change others! Perceive events and people differently, and that's what will happen.

We all must learn to make peace with ourselves and with others, I know, it's far from obvious, but it's important to reconsider the world around us, it's what it is, we do not We can change it, but what we can do is change our inner world, in order to attract to ourselves the right circumstances in our life.

Passing through phases of transitions enter childhood and adulthood. Every stage of our life changes environment, and above all, we change our internal frequency.

In reality, it is not the events that affect our perception of our environment, it is the interpretation that we make of it. The outside world is what it is, we can not change it in most cases, but what is possible to do is to reinterpret the vision we have of it, to redefine its inner world.

Try the following experiment, but I strongly recommend that you do not try to interact directly with those around you!

Train yourself to make positive affirmations in your imagination starting with what you love most in you, feel the beneficial effects of this first statement!

Then, reproducing the same feeling, you will think of something you like the least, and do this for one thing, I advise you something rather affordable, do not aim too high, because for your subconscious, what you think must stay in the realm of credible and probable. He must be convinced that this can happen.

Create the connection between the proven feeling for what you love most, and what you think of yourself in negative.

Learn to love what you hate, I warn you, it is quite destabilizing as a situation, because the connection is not really made, because you have been programmed for a long time not to appreciate you. But as you feel good about yourself by including the feeling of what you love the most, your mind will get used to it after a period of 30 to 90 days, if you do it regularly every day, it will gradually be included, and confidence will grow in you.

Change your angle of view, look at the outside world differently, get high and do not think about the inaccessible anymore! When you say that something is too expensive, you will never have the means to offer it to you, on the contrary, when you say that you have the means to buy everything that makes you want, it will happen, on the condition of erasing his old beliefs!

Do mental conditioning sessions to convince yourself! 20 minutes to 1 hour a day, you will not only imagine the person you want to be, but also, you will feel as such.

When you look at a house near you, what do you usually say? That you do not have the financial means. Now, I invite you to watch this same house several times a day if necessary, and to compare it with something that you can easily offer, such as a TV for example! What you have to do is a neuro-association between the feeling and the thought, and you will tell yourself deep inside you that what you can offer this house if you really want it. If you find that all this is absurd, it's just that you still live in your old pattern with your old dusty beliefs, it's all about a huge work on yourself and your old beliefs will not lead you nowhere if you continue to maintain them.

Do not aim too high at the beginning, go step by step, and gradually, seeing that what I tell you works, the belief will settle, then grow, then you can go to the next level.

9) Keep your interior tidy

Your cozy little nest is where you spend most of your time, so it is necessary to keep it in a pleasant state for yourself and for others.

The state of your home is a reflection of how your mind is, everything is disparate, nothing is clear, you find it difficult to find where you are, or where to start, in the end, you are discouraged.

10) Have an absolute faith

To have once absolute is this ability to detach oneself from all that we fear, and it is this that brings us closer to the materialization and fulfillment of your desires.

It's hard to think of two things at once, on the one hand, the prospect of earning big money, and on the other, to think about your debts, your thoughts must be genuine, that is, based on the real, from then on, you stay in the same pattern, conscious and very down to earth. Your desires must be part of your new reality, as if you had already obtained it, in short, you are the creator of your reality and the world around you, if you look at it differently, you will see changes happen.

Do not look at the obstacles! There will always be in life, and it is also adapt to all situations from outside, learn to ensure that it does not affect you directly.

Everything you experience from negativity despite the will to change are just jerks of your old beliefs, and the cycle is coming to an end to turn into something you desire, this is the law of Gestation, you must leave time to the best circumstances of your life, and during this time, try to keep a constant in your thoughts and in the ideal that you want to build.

What you must have in mind is only the destination, and sometimes, there are obstacles in life that allow you to get back on track, as strange as it may seem.

11) be generous

The universe gives and in abundance, but we must not forget that you are part of it and the energy is made to circulate.

If you do not give in your turn, the universe may be less generous towards you. Remember that you are a reflection of the world around you, and every individual you meet will remember you, and depending on whether you give it or not, you will not get what you want!

When you offer, do it heartily, it means there must be no expectation behind your donations, if you do it in the hope of getting more, it's as if you were in a pattern of missing because waiting also means that you do not have the desired object in your possession.

12) Do not worry about your problems anymore and look for solutions

Stop living in the pattern of worries about remaining problems and do not create any more! Create the circumstances of a better life without external parasites. When you are worried, you "create", it is you who strengthen the circumstances of what could happen to you.

Hope the best for those around you, because those around you have a negative influence on your morale, it is necessary to keep the least contact with these people for your good and theirs. And somewhere, helping them makes them dependent on you, and their problems become yours unintentionally.

Keep a healthy climate and without the problems crossing the threshold of your door, they must stay outside your home so they do not destroy the harmony you are trying to create.

13) be in action

Now that you have assimilated all the principles I have mentioned, all that remains is to take action. As powerful as the power of attraction can be, it requires an investment that goes in the direction of the desired goal.

I remind you, even if I have said it many times already, the magic is in you, and you are the architect of your life. We can not hope to see things appear in his life while waiting quietly in his corner, it would be too good.

A building is not built by itself just by thinking, it is necessary to create the circumstances to guide the universe about your intentions, and let him help you.

CHAPTER 9:
FOR FURTHER

"What we have to do to allow magic to take hold of us is to cast doubts out of our minds. Once doubts are gone, anything is possible. "
(Carlos Castaneda)

To conclude, I will highlight some points that seem important to you so that you can put all the tools in this book into application. Follow these last recommendations well, they will be precious to you.

Being in step with his reality

Do you know what happens when you fear that something will happen, or that you anticipate the behavior of those around you? For example, a car accident, the visit of a bailiff, the complaint of a neighbor, following a quarrel in your building.

You notice by your dismay that all that has been enumerated actually occurs, and if it works in the negative sense, why it would not be the same in the other direction?

Your mind is not used to anything other than the "catastrophes" scenarios of life and you vibrate at this frequency. This is high and the trigger is fear.

From childhood to adulthood, you have become an expert for negative manifestation to occur, and it still dominates your life.

Fortunately, there are positive manifestations, but they are more rare, and you do not know what process happened to you.

When we were kids, we were excited to open the Christmas presents, but this energy was lost over time, drowned in the difficulties of everyday life.

Our environment is the manifestation of what we have desired or feared throughout our existence. But there is one thing you can do to get life from everything what you want is to reconsider it or to see it differently.

If you want a new car with the intimate conviction that you will never have it, that's what it will happen, you'll have nothing, because your vibratory frequency is in no way in sync with what you desire. Saying it or thinking it is good, but do not forget that everything is energy and frequencies.

Above all, you need to be aligned at the right frequency, it's like you have to experience your desires on a Talky-Walky or a CB, but you're not on the right channel that puts you in touch with the universe .

What you need is finding the frequency for you to be aligned to the universe and you can interact and ask for what you want. Do not be confused about what you ask for, it is also necessary that the desire be clear and the message constant.

How to proceed ?

Take into consideration that everything around you is your universe and that you are the creator.

If you could draw the world with your hands, you would draw a round, besides, if you try to do it, you'll understand where I'm coming from! Join the two indexes above your head, then draw a circle with your fingers, saying "my world", redo it again with the feeling of creation.

Therefore, you are the creator of your reality, of "your world", and I would like to ask you this question: in this world, what would you like there to be? How would you like to see your surroundings? How do you value your life?

Be "the creator of your reality! ".

See the world as it is now, each person, and each object is only a reflection of your desires, you will not be able to change them directly, but you can have another look at them.

For example, if you wish to be lucky, you should not ask for it, but choose it, and anchor this new belief in you for a month, regardless of the external circumstances, they will diminish over time, just focus on that!

Your reality, the one you choose is that you are lucky! Shut up that latent thought of your mind, lie to you, and trust! Keep "faith".

In your reality you are lucky and it will manifest itself at any moment, only, it is necessary to let finish the cycles of the old schema. And I can assure you that it works! Believe it firmly! Make it your "reality", it's here and now!

Thoughts must be authentic

One must not lie to oneself, for to think of a desired thing without having the deep conviction that it will come will bring you nothing

The whole thing is to reach that sense of self-belief, and for that, you have to train your mind to aim for that goal, to think of a thing that has to be coherent and likely (that can possibly happen), your subconscious will accept it better. Therefore, try with a very small goal to achieve in a period of 90 days.

If you are aiming too high, here is what may happen, you will feel dizzy and nauseous, because something will not be in harmony with your subconscious, for example, aiming to have millions of Uros, trying to force the mechanism of your thoughts with something that is not in tune with your inner feelings, all that you will reap, it will be dizziness due to a confusion of the imaginary and the real!

In the first place, create the belief that what I am telling you works by doing little tests with something "possible", your mind will find all the solutions to lead you there.

hence the interest of starting small, the idea that you have (or will have) will be better assimilable.

It's as if you were going to an air-conditioned swimming pool, with an outside temperature of 40 ° C, the sun beating in full zenith.

If the water is at room temperature, you will get there without problems, and even you will dive, but if it has a freezing temperature, you risk a thermal shock.

On the other hand, by increasing the temperature of the water or if the air cools, it will become a little more bearable for your body, it will adapt gradually.

This is how your subconscious works, even if it does not accept the idea that seems to him incoherent, it is possible to make him accept in small dose.

To achieve your goals, you must stop dead with excuses and become more responsible. Everyone has this capacity if we give ourselves the means.

Be responsible for what you think!

When you imagine something improbable for your subconscious mind, it will whisper to you "it's a joke? ".

If you want a brand watch that is affordable to you, you will pay with no problem, with your money.

In terms of having the range above, you have to put the price on it, and this is where accountability comes in, can you afford it? This small step above you will be necessary for the continuation and your spirit will find the means to help you to reach there as far as possible, and without putting you in the difficulty.

What means will you use to obtain it?

What sacrifice would you be willing to make? Put money aside and ignore the superfluous.

This brand watch will come into your reality because there will be accountability, the intention and the authentic thought, the one that whispers that you can have this thing, it is almost within your reach, one more effort and you will get it!

The thought must be positive

Always keep healthy thoughts and tell yourself that you can do it.

In the case of the branded watch you envy, do not be in constant contradiction with yourself.

It is certain that if you tell yourself that you can not afford it, you will not get it! Establish your inner plan to achieve this, telling yourself that it will be possible (and it is!).

Put your inner action plan into place, keep in mind that this will happen because it's afford-able, putting money aside by making sacrifi-ces, working overtime, in the clear, get out of your comfort zone, otherwise, you will only dream of this watch.

You can do it, give yourself the means, be-come responsible, and walk around with what I could call "accomplishment," be proud of yourself!

This simple event in the form of a watch proves to yourself that you can go beyond.

Thoughts need to create new paths and it is up to you to direct your thoughts to the ultimate goal, incorporating steps, building the bridge between your current reality and the one you want! Create your interior plan!

Culture of the positive

Learn to maintain healthy thoughts, and without external interference!

Marvel at the world around you, and everything will be fine if you do it, do not live in fear of an event, anyway, it will happen, so what? Life is made up of ups and downs, but what matters in the end is the present moment.

Looking back, despite the negative events, there is one thing to remember, you are still alive! There are times when things do not go the way you want, but know this! These bad experiences motivated you to change course, and there were, after painful events, moments of intense joy.

So, whatever happens tomorrow, the day after tomorrow or in a month, stop being afraid, it only generates bad vibrations. And the more you will see the fear of seeing something happen, the more you will draw to you all the circumstances that will make it come true.

When the mechanism is launched, nothing can stop it, however, it is possible to mitigate the effects, pointing it to the positive, for that, I give you a sentence to say every day.

Note that it has more impact on a piece of paper that you keep in your pocket.

"Today is a good day, the best of all, and tomorrow it will be better and better! "

Use this sentence as much as you want, when you have a blow of depression and you want to give up because of external events, make abstraction for a moment, the time to say this sentence, take a step back and find refuge in your mind and regain your self-confidence!

The FIDI principle

It is a principle that can move you towards a better life, by overcoming all your blockages that prevent you from achieving a better life by reaching your goal.

What does it consist on ?

The initials FIDI mean "Force", "Interactions", "Determination" and "Intention or Investment".

To remind you, these are the same initials as the speech "F **! I'll do it!

In order to give you more information about the FIDI principle, I will dissect it for you!

First of all, "the Force", which is not necessarily linked to the physical condition, unless you turn to boxer or weightlifter careers.

The real force lies in his heart and in his head, we can speak of emotional force first of all, because many are hardened over time, who bear the best the hardships of life, and to have a mental capacity of bearing with all the difficulties with philosophy, not lamenting, but on the contrary being able to overcome the tests by seeing the positive side.

It is this ability not to fall back on oneself and endure all events without dramatizing and dealing with them.

We are all built on the same mold, the thing that has changed your inner strength are human interactions and hard knocks (as mentioned above)., We all have an inner reserve of strength that stays dormant.

And when you feel alive, you are able, you breathe, and you can behave in a certain way with the outside world, and most importantly, you can always stand up and show your true potential that ruminates within you.

The "Force" is also going beyond its fears and doubts to move forward to go from where the vulgar mount "F **".

Forget them "They say that," do it for yourself, if you have chosen a path, do not let anyone turn you away! Get started and no matter what you say on your back. Especially since the three quarters will not have the courage to do what you have undertaken.

Critics are the answers of the weak! Keep this in mind!

So go with your heart and your head and not compared to others!

Then, with regard to "Interaction", we all need it to move towards the path of success, unless we are like Karl Lagerfield's cat named "Choupette" who inherited his master's fortune without asking anything and without the intention of becoming rich, the only interaction was just meowing, and for you, you will need much more than that, it goes without saying.

Interactions are useful in society to make themselves known, meet friends or soul mate, or find the job of our dreams.

Imagine for a moment a world without Interaction, nothing would happen!

Do you want to get everything you want?

It must be expressed, everything can not be guessed. You will not see the girl of your dreams come to your house when she does not know you, or do not know your intentions, nor the boss of a company to ring at you, unless an incredible combination of circumstances, for you say "you start tomorrow! While he does not know you!

The only case in my knowledge or you will meet people without interaction will be when you give "dead letters" to reminders of payment, on that side, you will see a nice day landing a bailiff, and I doubt that it is this that you really want, and that will only bring you the negative (the reverse never having met).

"Interaction" is the "I" of "I'll" which means going, acting, or doing, the "I". can be too, "the intention of".

Concerning the "D" of "Determination", what does this term mean? It means clinging to your ideas, believing in your plans.

You want to succeed? Here is one of the essential ingredients, that of facing challenges, sailing despite the storm, not stopping in road.

To give you some examples of determined people, there are the sportsmen who do not give up in the face of chess, and wanting all the time to perfect themselves, the lost ones in the desert trying to advance costs that it costs until the civilization, or even me as a writer wanting to finish my book that can change the lives of thousands of people.
Determination is to keep a fixed point, a target, despite preconceptions and discouragements.

It is believing in one's projects and trying everything to lead them to their destination.

The "D" of "Do" means "to act in consequence, to be in action and to keep to the end.

And finally, the last "I" concerning "Investment"

How much are you invested in your projects? How much time do you spend on this one a day or a week? Unless you are among the velletic procrastinators, who constantly change your mind as soon as a difficulty arises, or if you feel that everything can wait. Arrived at the end of his life, we turn around and we say to ourselves "what have I missed as an opportunity in life? "

And yet, it is easy to invest and progress (I assure you that yes!)

By learning new things every day, watching videos on the subject, attending classes or reading books on the subject that deals with your project, focusing only on this same point, focusing all your attention on this one, you become better trained, a little more professional.

Do not wait until the results come right away,

but congratulate yourself on the progress you can make.

Always keep this same idea in mind, even if it seems complicated. Be curious, and if you are not, it is because you are not sufficiently invested in your project. There will be difficulties, moments of discouragement, but in any case, never give up, because that would sound your loss.

And the further you go, the more you will see it grow, the ideas one after the other becoming more specific in your mind, the image you will have will be sharper by including in the form an emotion, then several, you will have the perception of a new reality in your mind, this link between two worlds, on the border between dream and reality.

Your project is your baby, do not let him starve! Also, a baby can not be exchanged because it does not please you, in which case it would mean that you are not responsible enough.

On these words, I remember a game that appeared in the late 90s, it was called "Tomagoshi", a virtual animal that had to be fed. It was like an egg, and it was in the pocket.

Many people do not remember, because the poor virtual animal has surely landed in the bottom of a closet at home, starved to death.

Your investment is your "Tomagoshi", your "baby", and when we want something, it is our responsibility and our commitment to go through with it, otherwise we continue to zig-zag in life instead of going in a straight line (which is the shortest way).

The "I" of "It" in English symbolizes the object (the "it"), do you want it? So commit yourself!

To conclude on the "FIDI" principle, you have all the elements you need to move forward, and when an obstacle comes up against you, say "F **, I'll Do It! And no doubt many will ask me the question of why I do not put the word "F **" in full, because it is a book for all ages.

Power of creation
To try !

We will do a little experiment! (If your mind is ready for that!)

Put a glass of water on the table or another object of your everyday life! It will serve as anchor with the real world.

See yourself as someone who got everything he wanted, focus on this, and go around all that makes you want.

If you want a sports car for example, do not think about the financial aspect of it, or all around, just the car, focus, imagine the touch, the coldness of the metal , the texture of the leather, its color, everything, as if it were there, very close to you! Feel your hands on the steering wheel, feel the new interior of it and in your imagination, relax in it and feel all that relates to it, do you feel this inner joy?

I'll make a confession! What you thought about is happening! The object of your desires exists somewhere, just for you, and the more you focus on it, the more the object will materialize. It's rather exciting all that.

You do not believe in it ? So, that will not happen! And if in the bottom of you lies a latent doubt, it will not work either! It is necessary to attract to you all that you desire an absolute faith, without cheating, or ulterior motive, and I invite you to convince yourself really!

You will imagine owning this car and it is parked somewhere on a parking lot, and the glass of water serves to make the link between two realities yours, and the outside world.

Now, look at your glass of water, if it is real, the car is too, tell yourself this deep down inside you! Then look all around you with this sports car in mind, think of nothing else, why and how, just what you're thinking about.

Then, you will bring this car into reality, making the connection with a real object, such as a glass of water.

I recommend you to think about this car for several days, see, a month, this is part of your reality, it exists somewhere just for you!

At first, it's pretty dizzying because your mind will be in conflict, internally something will make you understand that everything you think is wrong, while on the other side, you imagine it's true. But over time, you will be fully convinced, thanks to the repetition.

Push your mind to convince you, without hoping that it will happen, or fix a date, just say that it will happen! That does not mean that, if you think of a car, it will wisely wait for you on the car park the next day, the universe will follow a process bringing you there by readjusting the trajectory of your current point to destination, the problems in progress will not stop like that, we must not dream, but it is imperative not to re-engage the process by telling

you "I'm out of luck! "It will never work! ", "
I'm totally useless ! », Etc. ... ..

CONCLUSION

We arrive at the end of this book, hoping to have given you many elements of answers.

As I said, this book has been designed in detail, being both accurate and complete. All the answers you've been waiting for are here, and if you learn to use all of the principles, at least if you start thinking about them, you'll see wonderful things happen in your life.

As you can see, there is only one magic, the ones in you, both the actor and the viewer, what you think of yourself and others created your reality, you are at the same time the mason and the architect, two forms of creators, the one that is in your mind and that draws the plans, and the other that lays down the materials to build the home of all your destiny. It is this notion that seems at once easy to apply, but difficult to explain because there are subtleties in the universe, but if you do exactly what is explained in this book, it will materialize as I do. I said at the beginning of the book.

Just one thing that all the authors in personal development did not mention to you, there is a counterpart and I really want to talk to you about it because it is very important! Do not be distracted by what will materialize as a shadow with green eyes called "Shakiman", according to a Celtic legend, she will visit you when you are at rest, she will wake you up and paralyze yourself by taking some of your energy, it's the price to pay and the risk, did I say it was safe? If I had spoken to you before, would you have always been tempted to know the secret?

But there is a parry if you do not want to have this visit (which may somewhat shock you), take something that will serve as a box, put a valuable item, the one you care most! A ring for example will do the trick! It is a form of sacrifice of your old life, then close it before midnight!

When you open the next day at the same time, you will discover something curious, the object you have deposited will be missing, however, there will be a note on which it will be noted something quite disturbing!

Would you like to know what is on it? I hope you will have a good heart, because some have struggled to recover! I tell you anyway, he noted on it, "Do you sincerely believe that a green-eyed shadow will appear to you during your sleep? », Did you have it right? (that he's teasing the author!)

Be assured! He has red eyes! (I'm still joking!), but if you do exactly what is said in this book (except the story of the box and green-eyed shadow a few lines above), this will happen, be sure!

In any case, I wish you all to succeed in everything you do in your vie thanks to this book, and do not forget! You are the only creator of your reality! And as Walt Disney said, "If you can imagine, you can realize it! "

friendly yours

Yoann MERITZA

SUGGESTIONS DE LECTURES

BOD EDITIONS

- GUARANTEED SUCCESS
Yoann MERITZA

- HOW TO REPROGRAM YOUR SUBCON-
SCIOUS MIND?
Yoann MERITZA

UN MONDE DIFFERENT

— RÉUSSITE MAXIMUM
Max PICCININI

— CONFIANCE ILLIMITÉE
Franck NICOLAS

— LAW OF ATTRACTION
Michael J. LOSIER

- THE SECRET
Rhonda BYRNE

EDITIONS BELIVEAU

— 7 ESSENTIAL INGREDIENTS TO MAS-
TER THE LAW OF ATTRACTION
*Jack CANFIELD – Mark Victor HANSEN –
Jeanna GABELLINI – Eva GREGORY*

POCHE MARABOUT

— THE COUÉ METHOD
Emile COUE

— THE POWER OF POSITIVE THINKING
Norman Vincent PEAL

MACRO EDITIONS

- YOU ARE BORN RICH
Bob PROCTOR

EDITIONS FIRST

- THE LITTLE BOOK OF THE LAW OF
ATTRACTION

Slavica BOGDANOV

HIDDEN TREASURE EDITIONS

- THE SECRETS OF A MILLIONARY
MIND
T Harv EKER

J'AI LU

— THE SECRET CODE OF YOUR DES-
TINY
James HILMAN

— COMPLETE YOUR DESTINY
Wayne W. DYER

— WHEN WE WANT WE CAN !
Normann Vincent PEAL

— HOW TO SUCCEED YOUR LIFE?
Dr Josephe MURPHY

— HOW TO USE THE POWER OF YOUR
SUBCONSCIOUS?

Dr Joseph MURPHY

— THE POWER OF WILL
Paul-Clément JAGOT

— THE GAME OF LIFE
Florence Scovel SHINN

— YOUR WORDS ARE A MAGIC WAND
Florence Scovel SHINN

— THINK AND GROW RICH
Napoléon HILL

— SECRETS OF COMMUNICATION
Richard BANDLER & John GRINDER

— BECOME A MENTALIST
Bastien BRICOUT

THE POCKET BOOK

— HOW TO MAKE FRIENDS
Dale CARNEGIE

— HOW TO SPEAK IN PUBLIC
Dale CARNEGIE

ASKA EDITIONS

— OUTWITTING THE DEVIL
Napoléon HILL

ADA EDITIONS

— SECRETS OF SUCCESS
Sandra Anne TAYLOR

- ATTRACT WHAT YOU WANT
Mélodie FLETCHER

BUSSIERE EDITIONS

— THE SECRET DOOR LEADING TO SUCCESS
Florence Scovel SHINN